Hidden Heads *of* Households

Hidden Heads *of* Households
Child Labor in Urban Northeast Brazil

Mary Lorena Kenny

Teaching Culture: UTP Ethnographies for the Classroom
editor: Rae Bridgman

Originally published by Broadview Press 2007

Library and Archives Canada Cataloguing in Publication

Kenny, Mary Lorena
    Hidden heads of households : child labor in urban northeast
Brazil / Mary Lorena Kenny.

(Broadview ethnographies & case studies. Urban series)
Includes bibliographical references and index.
ISBN 978-1-44260-084-3
(Previous ISBN 978-1-55111-792-8)

    1. Child labor—Brazil, Northeast. 2. City children—Brazil, Northeast.
3. Poor children—Brazil, Northeast. 4. Brazil, Northeast—Economic
conditions. I. Title. II. Series.

HD6250.B63N677 2007   331.3'109813   C2007-901735-5

We welcome comments and suggestions regarding any aspect of our publications—please feel free to contact us at the addresses below or at news@utphighereduation.com

North America
5201 Dufferin Street North York, Ontario, Canada M3H 5T8
2250 Military Road, Tonawanda, NY, USA 14150
Tel: (416) 978-2239; Fax: (416) 978-4738
email: customerservice@utphighereducation.com

UK, Ireland, and continental Europe
NBN International, Estover Road, Plymouth, UK PL6 7PY
Tel: 44 (0) 1752 202300; Fax: 44 (0) 1752 202330
email: enquiries@nbninternational.com

www.utphighereducation.com

Typesetting by Aldo Fierro.

Map on page 25 courtesy of blue_iq/istockphoto.com.

PRINTED IN CANADA

CONTENTS

LIST OF ILLUSTRATIONS

ACKNOWLEDGEMENTS

The writing of this book has been a journey that began in the summer of 1992, when I first went to Recife as a graduate student in anthropology. Since that time, many people have encouraged and supported me, and this work could not have been undertaken without them. Countless individuals provided information, insight, criticism, hospitality, and a sense of humor when I most needed it. They have all, in their own way, contributed to my understanding of life, Brazil, poverty, anthropology, and fieldwork.

I would like to thank first and foremost all of the children and their families that allowed me to write about their lives, especially Gloria, Edna, Dalva, Camila, and Demeris. I do not use pseudonyms. They have given me their consent to write about them and to publish this book about their lives. They have taken, and selected, most of the photographs in this book. I met them as children, and have maintained contact with them into young adulthood through multiple return trips to the area and through letters. Unfortunately, many of their hopes and aspirations have not been realized, and they continue to face significant hardship. I continue to learn about generosity, hope, and living life to the fullest from them. I dedicate this book to them, to those who have migrated to southern Brazil and Europe, and to those whose difficult lives have been tragically cut short through violence.

I would like to thank Dr. Russell Parry Scott of the Department of Anthropology at the Universidade Federal de Pernambuco in Recife for his support and encouragement, and to the university for granting research affiliation in 1994–95. Dr. Scott helped to keep me on course when I was tempted to go off on a million tangents in trying to understand the context of children's work in the area.

Many, many others fed me, housed me, and continue to guide my understanding of life among the poor in Brazil. I am now convinced that I gained some respect only when I stopped being sentimental about life in a poor community. When I first arrived, I trusted everyone, giving *feijão* (beans) to Luiszinho and *azeite* (oil) to Dona Gracinha, swaying and smiling from too much *cachaça* (rum) early in the day. I had opened my house as a place to rest and hang out, but on more than one occasion, I found people I did not recognize sleeping on the floor. I thank my roommate, Gisele, with whom I lived in that house for nine months, for teaching me about how to balance caution, optimism, and practicality. My immersion in the community was initiated and shepherded by her extensive network of friends and family. She was born and raised in a favela, and was streetwise, knowledgeable, and drew from an unending source of hope. Another neighbor, Bete Tavares da Silva, despite her disappointment in not being able to evangelize me, has always been a clear-headed friend who provided on-the-ground analysis of the dynamics of living in a poor community. Veronica Silva's spirit and lust for life is infectious and she continues to teach me about how to accept both the blows and gifts that come into our lives. Desperately poor, she has faced multiple bouts of cancer with such dignity, faith, and humor that it humbles me. Velhinha was an elderly neighbor known for chasing naughty kids with a block of wood. Her family consisted of a chicken that she carried in her arms like a baby, a multicolored bird, and a troubled dog that chased taxis. I feel privileged to have been included as part of her family. Dona Rosa, the mother of one of the children I interviewed, was in a perpetually depressed state whose origin she attributed to *macumba*, a spell put on her by an envious relative. My more materialistic diagnosis placed the etiology on poverty. I thank her and her family for sharing their home, always. Marcos, despite being a notorious thief and all-around *safado* (shameless person, trickster), was a self-appointed Robin Hood who would periodically treat everyone to food and alcohol after an especially "successful" day. I have no doubt that I benefited at times from his redistribution of goods. I thank Nedja's eight-year-old son, Pedro, who would bring me magazines about soap opera stars that he scavenged and ask me to pray with him before he slept. Dona Eremita, aged 70, was an elderly woman whose distinctive mark was her sheer red tops, shorts, and high-heeled shoes. She collected cans and stray animals, and took me under her wing because, she said,

"You pay attention to what I do. I think we are connected spiritually." She shared a two-room shack with her daughter, son-in-law, two kids, seven cats and a few dogs, all of which she took in from the street. She had a pig named *Sarney* (a former president) and a horse named *tubarão* (shark). Her favorite was a blind cat, which she kept in a stone cage. She frequently shared her pieces of chicken and bread with both the cat and me. Dona Ilda, an 80-year-old powerhouse, would shake her fist at intoxicated men coming home late from the local bars or yell at neighbors for channeling their raw sewerage into our area. During our late night conversations, she would smoke cigars and drink *cachaça* while we talked about the neighbors, their sons and daughters, what they wore, whom they slept with, who beat whom, how much money they had, or had spent, and on what, and what spells they used to prevent infidelity in their mates. She shielded me from harm after I accidentally killed all my neighbor's chickens, including the proud grey one, when they finished off the poison I put out for the rats. I thank Luiszinho, who early on appointed himself as my personal security guard, and would verbally assault visitors by demanding they pay a fee to see me. He acted as my human answering machine, taking messages from visitors when I was not at home, *for a price*, and would incessantly ask for advances on his expected Christmas, holiday, and birthday bonuses. When I would not pay him for his "work," he would invent stories about who had stopped by and what they had said.

Tobias Hecht and his wife Isabella provided meals, companionship, feedback, and much laughter on several occasions. Matheus Baccaro kindly gave permission to use his painting as the cover for this book. Since first seeing an exhibit of his work in 1995, I have been impressed by his ability to see and paint tragic urban spaces, such as favelas, with grace, sensitivity, beauty, and serenity.

Dr. Lambros Comitas at Columbia University provided consistent seasoned advice on research methods in anthropology. His humor, sensitivity, and experience guided me through more than one phase of rootlessness in Brazil. I am certainly indebted to him for accepting the collect calls from pay phones when I sought personal and professional guidance. Early in my career as a graduate student in public health, Dr. Rosemary Barber-Madden, a former professor at the Columbia University School of Public Health, whom I can now call a friend, always provided key insights about Brazil. She is someone I could count on to provide reality checks when my ability to focus on what is important would wane. Dr. Barbara Price has nurtured me intellectually and provided unfailing encouragement, hours of discussion, and fine-tuned advice at various stages of my writing. Her intellectual integrity and knowledge of the historical and contemporary political economy of Latin America provided me an indispensable orientation and a sober understanding of child labor.

I am grateful for the opportunity to write this book, and would like to thank Rae Bridgman, Anne Brackenbury, and Keely Winnatoy for their enthusiasm, feedback, and support of this project. Manuscript reviewers provided helpful criticism that has been essential in shaping its content.

The bulk of financial support for this research came from the Research Institute for the Study of Man (RISM) with a Landes Field Grant (1995). Other funders were the University of Miami, North-South Center, Program in Poverty and Urban Violence (1994), and Columbia University, Tinker summer field research grant (1992).

Special thanks go to numerous friends and family who have provided a wide and strong net of support for years, but some deserve special mention. My family has always been supportive and enthusiastic of my professional endeavors, even though I know I provoked anxiety on numerous occasions when I was negligent in maintaining contact while conducting fieldwork. Gina Bria has always reminded me of the true meaning of compassion, and continues to show me how to be in and observe the world. Marysol Asencio is an anchor in my life who, since we first met as graduate students in public health, has always provided invaluable opinions and moral support. Her deep consciousness and attentiveness to social justice are an inspiration to me. Thank you also to Audrey Charlton, Lisa Miller, Olga Gonzalez, Charlanne Burke, Kenny Broad, Jeanne Flavin, Nelun Wijeyeratne, Michler Bishop, Antônio Carlos Menezes da Silva, John Calderone, Mimi Cichanowicz, Laurence Hazell, Irene Glasser, Margaret Hynes, Linda Ippolito, and Leslie Kaufman, who are colleagues, friends, and kindred spirits who embrace and enrich my life with love, humor, and wisdom.

CHAPTER ONE
INTRODUCTION

We suffer a lot here. You are going to go away, but we stay.

—Rosemare, age 7

In 1994, soon after arriving in Recife, the capital of the state of Pernambuco in Northeast Brazil, I was walking in a heavily trafficked commercial district near the church of Nossa Senhora do Carmo when a crowd that had gathered around a small, thin boy accompanied by an adult male caught my attention. At first, it seemed as if they were doing magic tricks, acrobatics, or playing music. The boy sat on a towel on the ground while the older man talked and prepared the crowd for a performance. He told us that the boy would lie down on a blanket of broken bottles that lay a few feet from where he sat on the towel. Prior to this, the boy would put a sewing needle through his arm to show how impervious he was to pain. The boy then took a large sewing needle and pushed it through his upper arm. Most people in the crowd gasped and turned away as the pointed end of the needle came through the opposite side of his arm. After the needle performance, the older man walked through the crowd soliciting money. As people rummaged through their purses and pockets for change, one woman yelled, "I'm not giving any money until he lies down on the glass!" Others repeated her demand. The boy then lay on the glass, expressionless. His companion continued his solicitation, gathered some change, and the crowd thinned out. This type of "labor" is just one example of how a worldwide labor force of 250 million children between the ages of 5–14 work and help to support their families. Their labor contributes to regional and international economies, and global consumption.

In Brazil, over six million children between the ages of 10–17 and 296,000 children between 5 and 9 are working (Schwartzman, 2004, p. 122). An article in *VEJA* (Suor dos pequenos, 1995), a Brazilian weekly news magazine, stated that children produce much of what Brazilians eat, wear, and sleep in. About 60,000 children between the ages of 7–17 cut sugar cane in Pernambuco (Centro Josué de Castro, 1992/93). They harvest coffee and bananas. They pick oranges in São Paulo for the multitude of juice options we have. Employers like them because they are light and can climb trees without breaking branches (SEJUP, 1995). They pick cotton and sisal (jute) in Bahia for the rugs sold at places like the Pottery Barn (Buckley, 2000). They provide sex and drugs for foreigners on holiday and work in numerous bars and brothels. They break rocks in Santaluz, Bahia, and take care of the charcoal ovens in Mato Grosso. Kids dig tunnels by hand to find tin-ore, used to make tin molds for baking (Sutton, 1994). The "clay children" work in the brick furnaces in Piauí. They shine shoes in bus and train stations, carry luggage in hotels, wash and watch cars, work as maids, scavenge through trash for food and recyclables, and provide other low-cost goods and services. They glue the shoes that are part of a billion-dollar industry, with the US a primary importer. They work as weavers in the textile industry. The cacao, gems, minerals, soybean, and grape industries have all required the use of cheap (children's) labor. Medical assistance, work contracts, or security equipment are absent.

Children's work that allegedly does not interfere with school, such as work in the entertainment industry, summer jobs, "helping out" in the house and on the farm, rarely provokes the same level of pity or opprobrium. For example, in the neighborhood where I lived in upper Manhattan near the George Washington Bridge, children of immigrants sold fruits and vegetables, minded children, ran errands, and sold flowers, candy, newspapers, cigarettes, food, and drugs. My colleagues and I would shake our heads, say how awful it was that the kids had to work, and support campaigns on college campuses that discouraged the purchase of items made by children, but none of us knew anything about the children near the bridge, where they came from, or why they occupied a particular economic niche. Although we supported actions such as sanctions, fining companies that use child labor, and forcing businesses to pay for the schooling of the children who work for them, these actions never targeted the kids under the bridge, or the 800,000 children who harvest crops with their families in the United States (Association of Farmworker Opportunity Programs, 2005).

My interest in child labor in Brazil followed a three-month study in 1992, when I conducted research on the social networks of street children (*meninos/as da rua*) in Recife. Many labeled "street" children actually move in and out of homelessness, or work on the street during the day or on weekends, but are "attached" to families in some way. I was interested in the nature and extent of resources among those who severed ties or whose families abandoned them. Among those "attached" in some way to their families, I was astonished by their financial strategizing and humbled by their generosity. Fierce loyalty to family is often coupled with brutal consequences for not earning their keep. I often wondered why they did not just leave, or keep what they earned for themselves.

I returned to Brazil in 1994 to examine the context of children's work and the meaning this has for them, their families, and the community. Aggregate statistical studies on child labor homogenize the experiences of 17-year-old maids with 10-year-old sugar cane cutters, and I wanted to glean a more nuanced understanding of these young workers from their perspective. In general, children's perspectives tend to be overlooked or dismissed as unreliable because of their age. Adult views about children's work is skewed by their own notions about what constitutes "work" and the socially stigmatized yet much needed earnings of children. Class and race also contribute to their accounts being "airbrushed out of history" (Kundera, 1980, p. 3). Their status as poor and predominantly Black often means they are structurally inhibited from visibility and legitimacy. Their voices have also been inaudible because much of the labor they perform is illegal, seasonal, and opportunistic or, like women's work, unseen (Nieuwenhuys, 1994; Rodgers & Standing, 1981).

The Brazilian Constitution (1988, Article 7), and the *Child and Adolescent Rights Act* (ECA, 1990) prohibit work under the age of 16 (apprentices must be older than 14).[1] Hazardous or unhealthy work, working at night, and work that inhibits school attendance is also prohibited. However, the chasm between the law and everyday practice is wide. Laws and declarations that restrict child labor do not mean they are enforced or taken very seriously.[2]

One of the things that make enforcement difficult is the glaring and critical importance of children's earnings to the household. To those accustomed to an economy of surplus and the rearing of a relatively small number of children, adults who insist that their children contribute to household production are seen as abusive. Yet millions of families are faced with the daily battle of juggling scarce resources in circumstances in which any loss of income can be life-threatening. The closing of a sugar mill, factory, or restaurant, loss of a small plot of land or drought, or dismissal as a maid can be devastating to family income. This in turn affects what the family can eat and how children spend their time. Even if children combine work with school, they often "fill in" to compensate for lost wages of other family members due to illness, migration, births, marriage, and death. Safety nets such as savings, credit, private medical coverage, expense accounts, pension plans, free university tuition, and unions are non-existent. This is where labor and human rights standards clash with an individual's "right" to work, whatever their age. As Carolina Maria de Jesus wrote in her memoir, "the real slavery is hunger," not work (1962, p. 34).

In this book, I explore some of the complex conditions of child labor in an urban setting in one of the world's most poverty-stricken areas, where unrelenting scarcity shapes options, decisions, and worldviews. Numerous children graciously invited me to their homes, and allowed me to accompany them while they worked. With disposable cameras, they documented their lives. Most of the photographs in this book were taken by them. They were open about difficult issues, such as how the threat of physical abuse influenced their work. They continually taught me about research by challenging how I thought about issues and formulated questions. Early on, I was told emphatically, "You know, that's a really stupid question, 'What did you do yesterday?'"

Some of the children I discuss here I have known for over a decade. I met them in 1994 and have maintained contact until today, mostly through multiple return trips to the area and through letters. Many now have children of their own, and have "aged out" of the economic niches they occupied years ago. Their children will soon occupy the same positions they did, as little has changed in their lives. Some that I met in 1994 have migrated to the interior of Pernambuco, where agro-industrial growth has created a middle class in need of maids, nannies, and drivers. A few of the girls with "good" (straight) hair wait for it to become long enough so they can sell it. Others have followed family members to Rio de Janeiro and São Paulo in the hopes of securing work as a doorman, porter, or maid, while others anxiously wait for bus fare or news from the mother or father who promised to send for them once they were "settled." A few have fled, having been threatened by gang members for failure to pay debts, while two were shot and killed over disputes. One, whose greatest passion in life was soccer, was recruited by a soccer team in Rio. Many of the male *guias* (tourist guides), have met foreigners and moved to Germany, Italy, England, and Holland. They teach *capoeira* (a dance-like martial art developed by slaves), work as security guards, gardeners, or pick mushrooms. The girls I knew clean houses, and work as topless dancers in nightclubs. A few of the males have been deported: one for stealing everything in his partner's house after she left for work, another for selling drugs, and another for domestic abuse. A former tourist guide now has a lucrative business selling *nervosa* (crack), while others are addicted to crack, which 10 years ago had not yet penetrated poor communities in Northeast Brazil. Neto, who previously sold trinkets to help support his family, now sleeps in the cemetery and steals bicycles. "Hit men" show up at his mother's door to collect payment on debts, and threaten to paralyze him by shooting him in the spine. Another works as a "gun for hire." Janildo, who used to steal copper wires from phone lines to sell, has now joined *sem teto* (a homeless advocacy group). He is a squatter on unproductive land owned by a local Italian artist.[3] A few got parts as extras in the film *Amarelo Manga* by Cláudio Assis (2003), and received 60 *reais*, about US$30. Most of those I met 10 years ago continue to live in abject poverty.

Child Labor as a Social Problem

> We live and write history by a central tenet of nineteenth-century reforming liberalism, which tells us that one measure of a society's civilization and progress is to be found in its treatment of disadvantaged and dispossessed groups: women, slaves, and children. (Steedman, 1991, pp. 63–64)

Today it is widely considered a basic human right that all children should be protected from responsibilities that are dangerous or too burdensome for them. However, the notion that childhood is a period in which the only work appropriate for children is school work is historically recent. During the Middle Ages in Europe, the employment of children for long hours at low wages was the norm, and few thought the practice abusive because it was children, per se, who were employed (Nicholas, 1995, p. 1103).

Contemporary notions of childhood are seen as part of an evolutionary trajectory from a barbaric and brutal past that was ignorant of children's developmental needs, to a benign and enlightened perspective marked by "discoveries" of previously ignored periods of the life cycle, such as the peri-adult period called "adolescence" (deMause, 1974). However, research on the history of childhood shows that age-related norms are constructed within particular cultural, political, and historical contexts, not "mirrors" of an alleged objective measure of biological immaturity. Notions about what is normal, abnormal or "lost," what is in a child's "best interest," and the legal definition of a child, have shifted over time, oftentimes in response to changes in production, employment, consumerism, and human rights discourses.[4] For example, in the United States, the category "child" has previously included slaves, women, Native Americans, and the physically and mentally disabled (La Fontaine, 1986; Laslett & Wall, 1972).

The social historian Philippe Ariès (1962) is credited with producing one of the first major works on the historiography of childhood in *Centuries of Childhood*. Although criticized for using decontextualized and unrepresentative evidence (mainly from Europe), he theorized that the period we today call "childhood" did not exist prior to the Middle Ages. After age seven, children were considered "little adults." From the fifteenth to the eighteenth century, the notion of a separate and distinct phase of the life cycle (childhood) began to develop.

The writings of the Swiss-French philosopher and political theorist Jean-Jacques Rousseau had tremendous impact on changing ideologies about children. The publication of *Émile* in 1762 encouraged sensitive responses to the natural world, to animals, slaves, women, and children and advocated treating children as "a little human animal destined for the spiritual and moral life" (Boutet de Monvel, 1963, p. viii). According

6

to Rousseau, society corrupted the inherent natural innocence of children, and he reinforced the pivotal role of education in shaping the moral life of children (Robertson, 1974, p. 407).

Ideologies about children and childhood were bolstered by nostalgia among elites for a "natural and pristine" world that had evaporated due to the materialism and disconnectedness wrought by the Industrial Revolution and urban life. Industrialization and factories had radically changed production from primarily a domestic, rural economy to an urban-based one where the possibilities (and necessity) of remuneration outside the household increased dramatically. Although children's work in poor households has always been significant, even prior to industrialization (Steedman, 1991), industrial production eventually eclipsed household production, bringing changes in the division of labor. As opportunities for children as waged laborers in factories, mills, and mines expanded, so did their "value" (Harris & Ross, 1987; Haines, 1981; Goldin, 1981; Tilly & Scott, 1987).

In Brazil, children worked alongside their parents in the mills, and in urban areas, thousands labored in textile factories (Borges, 1992, p. 143). In Britain, factory owners preferred children to adults because they could pay them less for comparable inputs and productivity. Their smallness was a desirable characteristic for recruitment, since they often had to crawl under the machines.[5] Adults were frequently unemployed while their children were employed, and their earnings at times exceeded those of their parents. Parents came to rely so much on their children's earnings that they complained when child labor legislation (the Factory Acts of 1833 and 1883) restricted child labor (Smelser, 1959, p. 207). In Brazil, the minors' code (1926) restricted the age (14) and number of hours (6) children could work. In general, however, these laws were not enforced. Parents advocated for better working conditions for both adults and children, not the elimination of child labor. According to urban anthropologist Ida Susser,

> Nation-states, employers, and working-class movements define differently over time the categories of people available to work. As social programs and regulations shift, so too do the people who can be viewed as reserve labor. For certain historical periods, women,

> children, and the elderly have been legislated out of the
> work force. At other times, they have been recruited to
> fill employment needs. Such changes can be perceived
> in the history of laws about child labor, in protective
> legislation for women, and in the conflicting and his-
> torically fluid approaches of feminists, unions, and the
> state to such regulation. (1996, p. 413)

By the mid-1800s in Britain, the increased mechanization of production, child labor laws, laws protecting adult wages, and unions resulted
in large numbers of unemployed youth who were viewed as disorderly
and having "evil dispositions" (Davin, 1982, p. 635). Elite urban dwellers
demanded intervention by the state to curb these "menacing" packs of
idle youth (Hendrick, 1990, p. 39). The same kinds of fears about poor,
idle youth continue today. They are

> ... out of control, roaming the streets and indulging in
> acts of vandalism and violence.... In Abidjan, Bogotá,
> Cairo, Manila and Seoul, children playing in the streets
> and other public spaces and young teenagers congre-
> gating on street corners, outside cinemas or bars, have
> become synonymous in the mind of the general public
> with delinquent gangs. (Hoghughi, 1983)[6]

Subsequent legislation (1870s) provided a national system of basic,
compulsory education, which would effectively take them off the streets.
Other efforts to "police the poor" were implemented in public health,
law, and social work to curtail the "moral failure" among the poor that
reinforced their poverty.[7]

There have been numerous efforts to mitigate the use of children's
labor: laws restricting the age, type, and extent of labor; social welfare
(families paid a stipend to keep children in school); and penalizing companies that utilize child labor. "Indirect" measures include decreasing
fertility among the poor. This last approach gained momentum in the
late eighteenth century with the publication of Thomas Malthus' *Essay
on the Principle of Population* (1798). In this essay Malthus hypothesized
that out-of-control population growth would eventually outstrip the

food supply and that the poor, whose fertility rate was higher than the upper classes, should be encouraged to reduce their offspring. Riled by social reformers as blaming the poor for poverty, Malthus revised the essay in 1803 to include reforms (higher wages, education, insurance) that targeted raising the standard of living of the poor, not preventing their reproduction. These interventions, he concluded, would act as incentives to "naturally" reduce the number of offspring. There would be less need for children's wages and assistance in old age, as other financial "safety nets" would be available. Theoretically, the longer children remained in school, the more likely it would be that they could earn and provide for elderly parents (Grootaert & Kanbur, 1995, p. 194).

The International Year of the Child (1979) led to the founding of a number of child-focused non-governmental organizations (NGOs), conferences and workshops, and research studies. In the US in the late 1990s, the issue of child labor drew considerable attention when reports raised concern about US imports (carpets, sports equipment, agriculture, clothing, coffee) that use children as part of the production process. With technical and financial support from UNICEF, the World Health Organization (WHO), the International Labor Organization (ILO), NGOs, churches, and unions, numerous studies were conducted on the conditions of child labor worldwide (Rosemberg & Andrade, 1999).

In the following chapters, I attempt to describe the context and conditions of children's labor in urban Northeast Brazil. I first discuss the methods I used to understand these issues in one urban community. In the third chapter, I situate children's work in a complex social and economic history that has generated and perpetuated child labor. In the fourth chapter, I provide brief descriptions of various types of work children do and discuss how decision-making power and differential access to and distribution of resources affect well-being in the household (Beneria, 2003). Who gets what, when, and how much often mirrors larger societal inequalities. For example, adult males are often the source of authority, regardless of their irregular employment, lack of financial responsibility for children, or level of income earned by other household members (Safa, 1999). Census data based on the "head of the household" provides little insight on these internal dynamics.[8] Households are also "home" to non-kin, and children work in households for unrelated adults. Location, whether one owns or rents, is a squatter, is a long-term resident, or is a recent arrival, all are variables that provide insight into children's work. In the conclusion, I discuss projects and policies that attempt to help ameliorate the conditions that foment child labor.

NOTES

1. Brazil ratified the International Convention on the Rights of the Child in 1990. Since 1992, it has participated in the International Program for the Elimination of Child Labor (IPEC), a directive of the International Labor Organization (ILO).

2. Employers can be subjected to fines of over US$200 for violating child labor laws, but the fines are generally applied only after several violations (USDOL, 2002, p. 64).

3. *Sem teto* members are often at odds with *sem terra* (a grassroots landless workers movement) over squatter rights.

4. There are numerous studies on the history and historiography of childhood. John Boswell (1988) in *The Kindness of Strangers* examines the "redistribution" of unwanted children. Jacques Donzelot (1986) examines the effects of state intervention into family life since the eighteenth century. Linda Pollock puts absent children back into history and disputes Ariès' claims that children were just "little adults" with two volumes: *Forgotten Children: Parent-child Relations from 1500 to 1800* (1983) and *A Lasting Relationship: Parents and Children over Three Centuries* (1987). Joseph A. Hawes and N. Ray Hiner (1991) examine childhood from antiquity to the present, with case studies from 14 countries. In *Pricing the Priceless Child: The Changing Social Value of Children*, Viviana Zelizer (1985) explores the "value" of children over the past 150 years, and traces their status from economically productive to economically "useless," but emotionally "priceless."

5. A study by Levison, Anker, Ashraf, and Barge (1998) takes an in-depth look at the industries that employ children. They argue that "preference for smallness" is rarely a relevant variable for employment. Basically, employers can "get away with" paying children less than adults. Elinor Spielberg (1997) also found in her study of garment workers that preference for "nimble fingers" was not a factor in employment.

6. See also Muncie, J. (1984). *The trouble with kids today: Youth and crime in post-war Britain.* London: Hutchinson; Sumner, C. (1982). *Crime, justice and underdevelopment.* London: Heinemann.

7. See Lewis (1986) for a discussion of policies directed at developing a middle-class domestic ideal in order to preserve social stability.

8. See Harris (1984, p. 143), Whitehead (1984), and Wilk and Miller (1997) for discussions on the social construction of "households."

CHAPTER TWO
RESEARCHING CHILD LABOR

I hate researchers.
—Nilda, age 13

This was Nilda's response after I was introduced to her by the head of an non-governmental organization (NGO) working with street kids. She had just completed a survey with a North American public health researcher from Johns Hopkins University on abortion among street girls, and feared, I imagine, having to sit through another interview/survey. I was one of many foreign and Brazilian researchers interested in the lives of street children. Street kids tend to receive more attention than the "invisible" poor living in extreme poverty, even though their numbers are much greater. The splintering of street youth from "home" children provides them with the symbolic capital that journalists, psychologists, lawyers, anthropologists, charitable travelers, and NGOs seek (Bourdieu, 1984). According to a professor at the Federal University in Pernambuco, research on street children is sexy and "the middle class ideal of a good deed: it is, they believe, helping someone out and at the same time it is internationally relevant." In other words, the super-needy provide good copy. In 1992, there was heated response in the press over the dissemination of a research report on "sex trafficking," funded by UNICEF and the MacArthur Foundation, that showed the photograph of an alleged female "slave" for sale in a market in the Amazon. It was later revealed that the availability of the slave woman was a staged prank and completely unsubstantiated (Rosemberg & Andrade, 1999). One kid I knew was exasperated by reporters who refused to interview him because he was not an authentic *cheira cola*—a "real" street kid. Although he had been eking out a living on the street for years, he did not sniff glue and looked "too ordinary." I, too, searched for the "worst cases" (those who had completely severed ties with their families), as this was my understanding of "authentic" street youth.

The objective of my research in 1992 was to study the social networks of street youth, especially those that provide AIDS, HIV and other health-related resources and information. I had approached several social service agencies working with street youth and asked if I could volunteer with them and meet some of the kids. Responses ranged from lukewarm to mildly enthusiastic. All of the agencies I spoke with had had experiences with transient researchers who they felt were naive about street life and concerned only with their own research agenda. They were also reluctant to take on the responsibility of a "foreign woman in a dangerous situation." "What good is your research project to us?" Raphael, the head of *Grupo Ruas e Praças* (Streets and Parks Group), asked me.

> Look. I've seen my fair share of students needing data for their dissertations and research projects, as well as journalists who need catchy photographs. I'm tired of seeing these kids build relationships with researchers who, after they gather their data, leave without giving anything back to those who made it possible for them to do their work. This is just another form of Euro-American imperialism.

His assessment of the asymmetry between first-world researchers and third-world subjects was accurate. Over 30 years ago, the "crisis of representation" in anthropology questioned the power dynamic between researcher/observer and subject over who had the authority to represent and interpret culture (Clifford & Marcus, 1986). Although there is contemporary emphasis on egalitarian dialogue and shared authorship, there continue to be ethical issues concerning the role of professional mediators of culture and the stewardship of locals over representation. Social movements, post-colonial and cultural studies, and "electronic propinquity" (Appadurai, 1996, pp. 29, 44) have been powerful vehicles for shaping struggles over political and economic resources, cultural representation, and self-determination. Geopolitical relations, human rights and intellectual property law, and notions of nationalism, citizenship, and belonging also influence notions of who is a "native," an insider, and who has the right and/or power to represent.

Notions of insider/outsider often assume a homogeneity of thinking and behavior among those that share the same racial and/or ethnic, national, gender, class, and sexuality categories, ignoring the heterogeneity and power differentials among those of similar backgrounds. Sometimes, it was specifically my "outsider" status that made me safe to talk to, as I was not bound by the same types of relational obligations, responsibilities, and contingencies as my neighbors. Nonetheless, all representations and interpretations, whether from self-ascribed "insiders" or "outsiders" should be subject to critical examination of how information is produced, disseminated, and consumed.

Although I supported the efforts of social service agencies with street kids, I could not guarantee that my research would be useful or that my presence would not be a problem.[1] Despite the contemporary emphasis on anthropological reflection, and ethical obligation to do no harm, I had not fully anticipated my participation in this asymmetry until I was confronted by street kids exercising their right to informed consent. They asked where I got funding to study them ("Couldn't the money just come directly to us?"), what my objectives were, and what, ultimately, would happen with the information. Their sophisticated questions evolved from countless investigations by "transient information pimps," as we were called, who contribute little, they felt, to altering their situation.

Since that time I have met Italian psychologists investigating how "street socialization" affects child development, a British sociologist mapping the association between street children and crime trends, two other anthropologists examining "street youth culture," a North American law student on vacation looking for a way to defend the rights of street youth, and a young woman from the Midwest in the United States bent on saving street kids by putting them up in local hotels, giving them all her possessions, and then refusing to pay the hotel bills, claiming it was the "children's right" to be sheltered. One kid asked me to intervene and talk to the woman, as he found her behavior embarrassing and felt that the kids were taking advantage of her. Another time I was aghast as an aggressive graduate student from the US studying gender roles in Brazil pounded people with questions, which effectively coerced them into agreement. She asked a humble rural worker if he agreed that the "unspoken yet highly prevalent bisexual behavior among publicly heterosexual men was a reflection of the inherited patriarchal colonial system." The glassy-eyed, three-toothed, sandalled worker just looked at her and said, "I don't know."

Although the intent may be to "give them a voice" (as if the kids are waiting patiently for the researchers to come), the returns, according to them, are grossly unequal. Many feel their misery is used to fuel profits and advance the careers of both Brazilians and foreigners, and that there is little reciprocity or advocacy for those whose stories are appropriated. My roommate, Gisele, felt that "without favelas [shantytowns] there would be no politicians" and without *miseria* (destitution) there would be no researchers like me around. She found Michael Jackson and Spike Lee's 1996 music video "They Don't Care About Us," shot in Dona Marta, a favela in Rio de Janeiro, puzzling. Why do English-speaking foreigners want to dance to images of Brazil's poverty?[2] Rarely do subjects get to read or hear what is written about them, and for the most part, their lives go unchanged, which explains Nilda's comment to me at the opening of this chapter. They are suspicious about the motives of others in "caring for them" (Turner, 1993, pp. 3, 23). One street educator was bitter about the numerous foreigners who do their "stint" with street kids to fulfill a kind of sentimental solidarity and then leave.

> You know, most of this research doesn't benefit us. To tell you the truth, I don't like gringos; most of them just want to come here to have sex, to sell and use drugs, and do nothing, only have a good time. I met one foreigner who said she loved Brazil because it was so "free." Free meant she could drink when she wants, throw garbage in the street, urinate in public without getting arrested, and go through lights without stopping. Some just want to see misery and take pictures of it, and that's about it. Why don't you just let Brazilians help Brazilians! We have seen many like you, with good intentions, who try to get to know [the kids] and end up traumatized and very disillusioned.

Yet I also found young street dwellers who were eager to talk. Tiberius, Pericles, and Cicero would ask about street kids in the US, about the Iran-Contra scandal, the assassination of President Kennedy, the Ku Klux Klan, and why white police officers beat up Rodney King. "Would the same happen to us if we went there?" I told Cicero, aged 12, who occasionally engaged in *programas* (sex work) in the tourist district of Boa Viagem, that he shared the name of a famous Roman orator. "But I'm poor," he responded. "How can I be anything like that?" I was asked repeatedly why I returned to talk with them, since they thought their lives were too ordinary or unimportant to warrant attention. "Why the hell do you want to talk to us? Don't you have anything else to do?"; or "I'd like to have a job like that too." I said I wanted to find out about their lives so that I could tell people in the US about them. I think my presence was entertaining at best, irrelevant at worst.

My initial objective to carry out what I believed to be "action-research" (to deliver appropriate public health information) was quickly reconfigured by the children I met. AIDS, for them, was the least of their worries. Acquiring food, money, and immediate safety were their primary concerns. Even providing condoms proved to be problematic. One evening I accompanied outreach workers to distribute US-donated condoms to street kids. Before leaving, we decided to test a few. Our fingers penetrated all of them easily, and the rubber disintegrated in our hands. When we checked the fine print on the side of the box, we noticed an expiration date of three years earlier.

More than once, I was told to "stop hanging around and help make money." I watched as hunger led to desperation, then to violence. With a polite *"Com licença, eu tenho que arrumar alguma coisa"* (Excuse me, but I have to go "arrange" something), they would exit to go rob mostly elderly and female victims. It became increasingly hard to justify the usefulness of my research. What kind of "meaning" or action could I take that would effectively minimize their suffering or change their situation, besides band-aids of food and money?

This chapter opened with a quote by Nilda. Soon after making that comment, she was next to me, rubbing my hand on her belly, asking me what I thought of her protruding stomach. She was six months pregnant. She shot questions at me and did a good job of making me feel embarrassed and uncomfortable. She then told me she wrote poetry, and asked if I wanted to hear one of her poems. I agreed, hoping this would pave the way to a smoother interaction. "It'll cost ya," she said, and quoted me a price that included the current exchange rate for US dollars. If I wanted her story in order to fulfill my academic requirements, then I'd have to pay for it. She said the poems were based on her experiences living on the street. I include one of them here.

Whore
Everything began at my birth
It was torture, discrimination, and suffering
Hunger, thirst, rejection
And the most important thing that I wanted
I didn't have:
Respect from people

I was raised and I raised myself
In the streets wandering around
Marginal, prostitute, drug addict, thief
These were all the assertions
That everyone in society would believe true

Without knowing
I lost my virginity without wanting to
I was beaten, raped, and a child
From this act would be born
And one more time I would believe
That this mistake wouldn't happen
My reaction was to want to die

Clean city, empty land
I am suffering, because I am alone.
Prohibited, thrown away
This is our life history.
(Translation mine.)

I returned to Northeast Brazil in 1994 to examine children's work within the context of their family and community. A single, universal definition of "labor" is difficult, as the state, employers, parents, and children do not agree on when something is work and when it is just "helping out." I found a useful definition of children's work in Enid Schildkrout's (1981) study of Hausa-speaking Muslims of Kano, Nigeria, where male and female children serve as vital links between women in purdah (seclusion) and the outside world. Women are able to maintain their income-producing activities because children carry out most of the tasks. According to Schildkrout, a definition of child labor should include anything children do that contributes to production, frees or facilitates the work of adults, or replaces the employment of others. I also decided to focus mainly on children under the age of 14, as labor under this age was prohibited by law.[3]

Although I had numerous informal, spontaneous conversations about children's work, I also conducted structured, in-depth interviews with about 10 children and their families. These interviews were not conducted until almost the end of my year in Olinda, after I had developed deeper relationships with a few families. (See Appendix A for a sample of questions.) I conducted life histories in order to assess how school, births, deaths, illnesses, and so forth contributed to changes in children's work (Hareven, 1991; Young, 1986). People rarely speak of their lives chronologically (despite my efforts at imposing this). Rather, seasonal and cyclical events, such as Carnival or São João, or significant events such as "before I was pregnant," were the hubs of their stories. Life stories are always works in progress, and they grow, change, and decay over time. Since life histories are living things, some children I met years ago had revised what they said earlier, or no longer emphasized things that were once important.

All structured interviews were tape-recorded and conducted without a fixed monetary payment. However people could consistently count on my giving them food, money and help in an emergency, which has continued until the present. In turn, I was given assistance—food, emotional support, and companionship—in more ways than I can count. Information was also gathered from other researchers in the area, social welfare agencies, and newspapers.

All of these children work in the "informal" labor market. It is illegal, "hidden," and unrecorded in official statistics. Labor studies generally exclude the elderly (over 65) and those under 15 as non-working household members. Thirty years ago anthropologist Keith Hart (1973) used the terms "formal" and "informal" to describe and differentiate income earning opportunities in Accra, Ghana. The International Labor Organization (ILO) then popularized the use of these terms to describe a dual labor market, one that is state regulated, and one that is unregulated, opportunistic, and includes "family" labor. There are debates over the applicability of this rigid dichotomy in describing types of labor, as well as the assumed benefits and desire for "formal" labor conditions. For example, difficulties in providing mandatory contributions by both employers and employees creates an incentive to seek informal contracts (Gill, Montenegro, & Dömeland, 2002, p. 83).

During my initial year of fieldwork (1994–95), I resided in a poor, working-class neighborhood that allowed for multiple contacts with kids who would stop by mostly to eat, but also sleep, take showers, do their nails and hair, and talk. Many of the interviews I conducted took place on the floor of my kitchen. Other "draws" to the house were a *boca de fumo* (literally "smoking mouth") behind the house where marijuana was consumed and distributed. A pay phone was located outside my front door, which, to my dismay, drew people 24 hours a day to hang around, make calls, fight, meet lovers, and knock on my door soliciting *fichas* (telephone coins). There were periodic shootouts between rival gangs, between police and gangs, between lovers, and between family members. Not unlike my neighbors, I was the victim of muggings (twice), had my house broken into twice as well, and had my clothes stolen off the laundry line in the back. Unfortunately, I lost a lot of clothes before I figured out that no one left their clothes on the line after dusk. One of the break-ins was committed by an intoxicated, self-ascribed "artist" who was angry with me for not purchasing his surreal sculptures and who called me an American imperialist.

Being tall, white, middle class, female, single, childless, and from the United States set me apart from locals in a number of ways. By some, I was perceived as a wealthy *gringa* (foreigner), and it was expected that I would become a *patroa*, someone who could provide material and other aid usually in exchange for labor. One of my Brazilian friends cautioned me.

> Look. Don't think people hang around because they
> really like you. I mean you are not a bad person, but
> I would advise you not to tell people why you are

here. Tell them you are just passing through, a tourist. Otherwise, they will think you work for a company
or organization, and can get them money. They will
fill your head with things to see and do, and then hit
you up for some cash. And don't be too friendly with
the neighbors. All they want is to know your business,
in detail. I know you want to live among the "people,"
but don't kid yourself. A fishing village is the people.
Where we live is dangerous. Don't think that because
they are nice to you, they will not show up at the door
with a knife in hand.

For a time it was rumored that I was spying for the FBI or CIA because
I asked so many questions and did not have a "real job." Others told me
my research topic was just one more example of the US misrepresenting
and discrediting Brazil, or pornographically putting Brazil's tragedies on
display, what Langer (1982, p. xi) referred to as "tillers in the field of atroc-
ity." Still others thought I was a drug trafficker, padding my bank account
with drug money and distributing credit cards to my informants.

I was "studied" as well, watched to see who came and went in the house,
whom I associated with, and what my reactions were to certain issues. As
a single female hanging around young children, I was also seen as a potential kidnapper, looking for stray children for wealthy infertile couples
and for those needing organs. This perspective was fueled by rumors that
began in the mid-1980s that poor children were being kidnapped and
sold to foreigners for their body parts (organ theft or harvesting) under
the pretense of adoption (Scheper-Hughes, 2000). There were posters in
offices, clinics, and bars showing a child with its body parts priced like
a cow in a butcher shop: US$1,000 for eyes, US$5,000 for arm bones,
US$5,000 for the heart, US$20,000 for the kidney, US$10,000 for the feet.
Benedita da Silva, the former Secretary of Public Welfare and Promotion
under President Lula, stated in her memoir that

the majority of the babies are being sent to Italy,
France, and Canada. The babies are taken out of Brazil
with false passports. The illegal export of babies is a
lucrative business; I've heard that the traffickers can

get $25,000 to $30,000 per baby. Four-thousand police stations in Brazil have filed reports of children disappearing mysteriously. There have been many cases of children disappearing from hospitals and we suspect that some hospital workers might be involved in this trafficking of babies. These disappearances have fueled rumors [of] ... networks in which babies are illegally exported overseas, where their organs are used for transplants. We know that there is a strong demand for these organs overseas. (1997, p. 156)

The "common-sense" logic that expresses both fear of exploitation and conspiracy is common where disparities are extensive (Gordillo, 2002). According to Scheper-Hughes, "If Brazilians and other Third World urban poor think that agents of the privileged want to attack and mutilate them, isn't this basically so because it is true?" (Scheper-Hughes, 1996b, p. 33). In 2003, 11 impoverished men from Recife, Pernambuco, sold their kidneys through an Israeli broker. Their kidneys were used for transplants that took place in South Africa, in one case for a recipient in the United States ("Brazil arrests 11," 2003; Rohter, 2004). Concerns about the commodification of poor bodies was also reflected in life history interviews I conducted in 2002 and 2003 with survivors of a 1932 *campo de concentração* (concentration camp), who had been "corralled" in a camp as a drought mitigation strategy in the interior of Ceará. Narratives contain recurring references to adulterated food, haphazard disposal of the dead, and organ harvesting. In fact, as part of the yellow fever surveillance program directed by the Rockefeller Foundation (1923–40), obligatory sampling of liver fragments were obtained through postmortem viscerotomy (Löwy, 1999) with a viscerotome or "liver punch" (an external tube and a sliding steel blade (Löwy, 1997, p. 134). In the rural interior where doctors were rare, representatives—be they pharmacists, gravediggers, or registrars in the vital records office—were contracted by the Viscerotomy Service and received a fixed sum for each liver specimen submitted. They received a bonus (100$000—one hundred *mil réis*, about US$7) if the specimen was positive for yellow fever. Laboratory staff reported a substantial number of non-human (pork, dog, goat, and cow) submissions, as well as liver fragments from the same person submitted under different names. Fragments were also taken from those who had not died from "the fever" (fatality within 10 days of onset) (Soper, Rickard, & Crawford, 1934; Hamilton & Azevedo, 1999; Löwy, 1997, p. 135). These caused camp residents to feel that even after death their bodies were commodified.

It takes a significant amount of time to have a clear idea about what kind of work children do, and how they talk about it. I could not ask them about work without knowing first how or if they saw their work as a "problem" to be investigated, how they saw themselves in relation to other children, and where their work was placed in relation to other concerns in their lives. Only then could we discuss what they thought could be "done" about it. Child labor is not an objective "thing" to be studied, but constructed within a web of relationships. For example, emphasis on the violation of child labor laws was never important. What was important was the impact of their earnings for their family, the role they assumed in their family, how resources were allocated, changes in work and opportunities, and other daily stresses and hassles they faced, such as figuring out how to pay a dentist to get a new tooth, owing money to *agiotas* (loan sharks), declining physical and mental health of family members, and discrimination. Overall, the axis of meaning from which everything branched out was their family. The history of their work, then, was really the history of their family. What was "right" was to be seen as hard working and selfless. The discrepancy between political rhetoric about eliminating child labor and what they expected to happen in their lifetime was significant. Most did not expect very much to change.

NOTES

1. The main objectives of *Ruas e Praças* was to organize street kids into *nucleos de base* (street youth collectives). Through group activities (soccer, retreats, agriculture, painting, sewing, workshops) the kids were encouraged to develop a reflective "consciousness" about their position, modeled after Paulo Freire's theories on *conscientização*, a method of problem-based literacy education, critical thinking, and praxis that emphasizes awareness of the socioeconomic and political roots of inequality. Group identification, solidarity, and political mobilization

would be fostered by this critical reflection. During my short stay (three months) in 1992, there were at least five demonstrations organized on behalf of street children in Recife, and two nationally.

2. Jackson, Michael. (1996). They don't care about us (Spike Lee, Director). Referenced in Barke, Michael. Samba: A metaphor for Rio's favelas? *Cities, 18*(4), 269.

3. In 1999, the minimum age was raised to 16.

CHAPTER THREE
SITUATING POOR CHILDHOODS

Figure 3.1: Map of Brazil

B razil, the fifth-largest country in the world, ranks as one of the most powerful and dynamic economies in Latin America and among the largest in the world. Yet extreme income inequality (the poorest 20 per cent account for only 2 per cent of national income), racism, and violence perpetuate significant disparities. Over 25 per cent of the population lives on less than $2 a day and 13 per cent live on less than $1 a day (World Bank, 2005).

In Northeast Brazil,[1] over 50 per cent of the population is classified as poor. Five hundred years ago, this region was the political and economic hub of Brazil. Brazil was the most important sugar producer in the world, with coastal plantation agriculture dependent on indigenous and then slave labor. Trade in sugar, gold (eighteenth century), coffee, rubber, and cotton (nineteenth century) created a nexus of power concentrated among a small group of linked elites that included large landowners, politicians, police, the judicial system, and the church (Ribeiro, 2000). By the end of the nineteenth century, the vestiges of these trades—freed slaves, abandoned children, and poor immigrants—were eking out a living in the countryside as sharecroppers or squatters on abandoned *latifúndios* (large estates), or as *biscateiros* (day laborers) and beggars in the urban areas. The poor significantly outnumbered the wealthy Portuguese colonizers. Besides the Catholic Church, few institutions addressed the exigencies of the poor (Schwartzman, 2004, p. 17). After the establishment of the Republic in 1889, the state increasingly assumed responsibility for the poor.

Periodic drought in the Northeast causes significant loss of life, livestock, food, and work, and has historically forced thousands into the urban capitals (Villa, 2000, p. 13). In the early twentieth century, the influx of masses of poor scavengers into urban areas led to programs such as segregating drought refugees in encampments, or forcing them to relocate to less populous areas, such as Amazônia (Neves, 2000, pp. 27, 145). These programs mirrored both the symbolic and spatial divisions between a minority of white, urban elites and *matutos* or *caipiras* (derogatory term to describe those from the rural interior, equivalent to the use of "hick" or "country bumpkin" in the United States),[2] who were seen as backward, ignorant, and superstitious, ultimately preventing Brazil from "modernizing" (Neves, 2000, p. 222; Sousa Rios, 2001, p. 40). Interventions were guided by a "scientific" racial ideology of the day that asserted an association between poverty, race (biology), and culture (Neves, 2000; Chalhoub, 1996, p. 29; Albuquerque, 1999, p. 144; Löwy, 1997, p. 125; Jackson, 1994, p. 90; Villa, 2000, p. 69; Neiva & Penna, 1916; Carvalho, 1992, p. 20). "Culturally primitive" dark-skinned persons were "less fit" than "vigorous whites," prone to sickness and moral depravity. National strength depended on both physical and moral "hygiene." Europeans were subsidized to immigrate to Brazil both to meet labor shortages in the coffee plantations in the south and as a eugenic strategy to promote "good" genetic quality and a biologically and culturally "healthier" (whiter) population (Neiva & Penna, 1916, cited in Blake, 2003; Chalhoub, 1993, p. 459).

Until 1930, poverty was considered unfortunate, but natural and inevitable, anchored by a structure of paternalistic "unequal reciprocity" (Neves, 1998, p. 53). With increasing federal power after 1930 and implementation of state welfare programs such as public housing, hospitals, and recreational and educational institutions, dependence on the "good will" of patrons declined. Immigrants organized cooperatives, labor unions, and political parties. The Ministry of Work, Industry and Commerce was created and developed codes and standards protecting the labor of minors, as well as laws protecting worker rights such as paid vacations, workers compensation, pensions, and health benefits.

In the late 1970s, after a 20-year military dictatorship, the *abertura* (opening)[3] allowed a proliferation of non-governmental organizations (NGOs) with various social, economic, civil, and political agendas to develop. According to the Brazilian Institute of Geography and Statistics (IBGE), there are now a half million NGOs in Brazil (IBGE, 2004). There are high expectations that NGOs will address issues neglected by the state, regardless of their limited capacity to change laws, or implement policies and reforms that hamper elite interests, minimize inequity, or empower the poor. Some NGOs are criticized for "recycling the old oligarchies" (Araújo, 2004, p. 37), and replacing the rural *coronel*[4] as a "super-patron" (Da Matta, 1995, p. 44). A lack of transparency, top-heavy administrative costs, pet projects, and a lack of participation by those they represent are also issues that have inhibited the impact of NGOs (Sorj, 2005). Some NGOs are threatened by drug traffickers for their involvement in community-based projects that focus on "taking back the community" (Sorj, 2005, p. 33). Finally, NGO autonomy is circumscribed by the interests of international funders who have their own notions of what development, empowerment, culture, and citizenship mean. For example, in May 2005, a coalition of Brazilian groups working on AIDS outreach, education, and treatment rejected $40 million from USAID (United States Agency for International Development) because of a clause that prohibited them from working with prostitutes.[5]

One cannot overlook how elites engage in their own forms of "reciprocity" through bribes, favors, laundering of money, and tax evasion (Souza Martins, 1994; Pinheiro, 1996). Corruption is an issue that Brazilians across all classes chronically lament and feel powerless to change. A study by the Getúlio Vargas Foundation concluded per capita income would increase by US$3,300 if corruption were eliminated (Abrúcio, 2000). A taxi driver in Recife provided his own analysis of corruption.

> Here one has to suffer, deal with corruption, and learn how to take advantage of other people. We know what the problems are, how to make formal complaints, but whoever opens their mouth is going to end up dead. The people who do open their mouths are the true heroes in this country. Chico Mendes only became a hero after he was dead.[6]

Despite the proliferation of NGOs, many citizens continue to rely on patrons for loans, help with medical emergencies, to navigate bureaucracy, get a job, a bed in a hospital, and legal assistance (Da Matta, 1995). The continued reliance on patrons perpetuates "unequal reciprocity" in which "desperation can be called loyalty and exploitation can masquerade as care and nurturance" (Scheper-Hughes, 1992, pp. 111–12). Many rely on the campaigns of political candidates who are notorious for handing out food baskets, medicine, wheelchairs, and school scholarships, as well as paying for tubal ligations, funerals, and light and water bills in exchange for votes.[7] Political rallies are usually festive events, and regardless of what one thinks of the candidate, people often go just to take advantage of what is given out for free. One afternoon while we watched a mayoral candidate arrive on his *trio electrico* (flatbed truck mounted with loudspeakers and bands), my neighbor commented,

> Did you know that the government gives out free sterilizations during election time? And food? And T-shirts? Most women do not know what is happening. Politicians offer it free, to get votes. Women make the decision just because they are having a hard day. They don't know anything about the candidate, not even their name, unless they get a free T-shirt with the name printed on the front. Most people don't even know how to form an opinion about someone because they are

illiterate or feel inferior or that they don't know anything and therefore have nothing to say. Candidates
basically buy people, and candidates have to. You know
why every Tom, Dick, and Harry wants to be a state
deputy or city councilor? Because you'll end up with a
house, your light, gas, and water bills paid for.... Now it
all looks like a big wild party, and unfortunately for us,
there is really nothing serious going on. Beyond this
rally most candidates don't even want to come near
poor people.... This is just the way things are done here
... I want my *cesta básica*.[8]

More importantly it is fear—of revenge, of losing a job, of being accused
as subversive or disloyal—that silences demands for social and economic
equality. "*Quem tem dinheiro, anda bem. Quem é pobre aqui, dança*," said
my neighbor, meaning it is the poor here who dance to someone's tune, do
what they are told, act in accordance with the rules. "I don't know where the
reciprocity part comes in. The poor here only have obligation, and pretty
much feel that they should only do what those above them tell them to do."

POVERTY AND GLOBALIZATION

"Globalization" is a process that is differentially understood and experienced. Some scholars view globalization as a new label to describe
processes previously defined as "development" or "modernization"
(Edelman & Haugerud, 2005). According to David Harvey, the term
became ubiquitous after 1970 when American Express used it to market
its credit card (Harvey, 2000, pp. 12–13). Empirical studies question the
notion that globalization is an ineluctable "force" with homogeneous outcomes (Castells, 2000, p. 165). The effects of structural adjustment polices
(currency devaluation, wage controls, and cuts in health care, education,
family planning, and sanitation), and neo-liberal policies (privatization of
utilities, transportation and banking) that rely on the market rather than
the state to address socioeconomic problems have had varied outcomes
across the globe. Although there has been a global increase in wealth, a drop
in infant mortality and increase in life expectancy, inequality and poverty

have deepened in some locations, especially Africa. The expanded trans-global flow of communications, capital, labor, and production (primarily a search for cheap, unorganized, unregulated labor and the evisceration of labor laws and protections) and consumption are differentially experienced. Some groups benefit from the increase in wealth, power, and access to information, while others are socially, spatially, and economically excluded in "black holes" of structural irrelevance (Castells, 2000, pp. 165–68).

Global shifts in production, consumption, and investment have had significant consequences for labor conditions, land use, and access to resources in Brazil, resulting in the growth of urban favelas and regional differences in development. In many cases, technology and "modernization" have led to more entrenched wealth and inequity. Although per capita income has increased, development and quality of life across regions and classes are uneven. In many areas, poverty has deepened. The states with the most dynamic economic growth in the Northeast are also those with increasing concentrations of wealth, challenging the assertions of a "trickle-down" model of development common in neo-liberal economic policies. The area continues to exhibit the most negative profile of social and economic indicators in the country (Beserra, 2004, p. 9). Although infant mortality declined from 151/1,000 in 1970 to 80/1,000 in 1988, it is still three-quarters higher than the national average (Araújo, 2004, p. 34). Life expectancy (58.8 years) is the lowest of all regions. Caloric intake (as a variable in measuring standard of living) rarely meets nutritional need.[9] The poor survive on cheap, empty calories such as rice, black coffee, and sugar. High-calorie sugary foods (soft drinks, candy, sweet rolls) *matar o fome* (kill the hunger, fill you up) quickly, despite their lack of nutritional value. Hunger interferes with concentration. Ten-year-old Lena would sound almost apologetic in telling me why it was difficult to concentrate in school. "The hunger gets to me. I am not very strong. I can't stand it. Sometimes even after I eat, the pain is still there. My stomach hurts from the hunger. Sometimes I can't sleep, I'm so hungry." Malnutrition also stunts children's growth. I was always shocked when what I thought were 10-year-olds turned out to be 15-year-olds. Unemployment is also higher than the national average and per capita income remains the lowest in Brazil.

Among the poor in Olinda, working only one job is rare. Many adult males work as *biscateiros* (day workers), hired to paint a house one day, clean a yard the next. Some have "regular" work washing cars behind the post office, or selling peanuts and ice pops at the beach. Adult women work as laundresses, or secure part-time work as a hairdresser, manicurist or seamstress. The most common source of waged employment for a poor adult female is working as a maid for families living in the wealthier areas of Olinda or the convent. The market for maids is saturated, even though many employers do not provide legally entitled benefits. One woman who worked for a family in the Cidade Alta told me, "Most maids have no idea what they are entitled to, what they are supposed to get. And if your employer dismisses you, they can always get someone else."[10] Women also run small *barracas* (stands) selling meat, milk, eggs, canned goods, rice, and beans. They sell cakes or resell clothes, do hair and nails in their home, and sell makeup. They take care of other children in the neighborhood and raise chickens. Income is often supplemented by an elderly relative's social security benefit. Life histories show that parents started working at the same age as their children. According to Bete, age 41, and mother of seven, "When I was eight years old I was already working in other people's kitchens, just as my mother had done before me. Now, my kids are growing up with the same routine, working to help me."

In the last 20 years, growth in the Northeast has occurred due to capital investments in factories that produce soccer balls, shoes, and clothing in a region of the country where labor is cheap, labor laws are not enforced, benefits are few, and tax incentives are many. Due to zoning regulations, Pernambuco's participation in this growth was less than other states. Exports fell from 30 per cent in 1975 to 8 per cent in 1980 (Araújo, 2004, p. 31). Due to this "incomplete industrialization," a large, unskilled labor force is without any kind of social safety net (Pino, 1997, p. 22).

Until the 1930s, those in the "interior" (referring to the countryside) outnumbered those in urban areas. Small farmers, sharecroppers, and tenants (who do not own the land) would sell their meager surpluses of corn, beans, and manioc. Today, their diets are increasingly made up of purchased canned or packaged goods, rather than food they grow themselves. About 25 years ago, Brazilian agriculture underwent a major transformation. Increased mechanization and agro-industrial, export-oriented production, and the increased hegemony of cattle raising (which requires large land masses but few laborers and produces no food) decreased the demand for labor while swelling land concentration, as small farmers sold their plots of land. The safety nets provided by rural unions in the 1970s eviscerated due to debt. These processes led to massive rural emigration to the south and coastal cities (Araújo, 2004, p. 24). Other transitions, such as the decline in the price of sugar over the past 20 years, and an increase in the use of artificial sweeteners, reduced demand for refined sugar (Wolford, 2004, p. 154). In Pernambuco, 14 sugar distilleries (*usinas*) and mills (*engenhos)* closed. Recent droughts also exacerbated vulnerability, and thousands of workers have left in search of work in urban areas (Menezes, 2004). Those who remain in the interior survive on the meager social security benefits of relatives, which are rarely above one minimum wage (about US$133/mo)[11] or rely on remittances from those who have migrated to the city.[12]

According to the 2000 census, the majority of the 169 million Brazilians live in urban areas. In the Urban Regional Metropolitan Area of Recife (RMR), 63 per cent of its 3 million residents are considered poor, with half working in the informal economy. About a quarter of the population live in one of the 600 favelas in the area (Pontes & Schmidt, 2001). About 90 per cent of the favela population makes less than one minimum wage (300 *reais*; US$133/mo). The number of hours one has to work to buy food keeps increasing. In 1960, 25 per cent of the minimum wage was spent on a *cesta básica*; today it is 65 per cent (DIEESE, 2005). The minimum amount needed to cover the necessities of food, rent, transportation, hygiene, education, and insurance is about eight monthly wages.

COLOR AND WELL-BEING

Brazil began to import slaves in 1530 and in the course of over 300 years imported more slaves than any country in the Western Hemisphere (40 per cent of all slaves sent to the Americas). It was the last country to abolish slavery (1888). It has the largest population of African descendants outside of Africa (almost half out of 183 million people).

Since the 1930s, scholars generally concurred that the African diaspora in Brazil was situated within a unique "racial democracy" (Freyre, 1946; Wagley, 1969). Stratification was asserted as class-based, with a large *mestiço* (mixed) population given as evidence of nondiscriminatory miscegenation (Pierson, 1967; Bastide & Fernandes, 1971, pp. 229-68). This differed from the institutionalized segregation and racial tension found in the US (Jim Crow laws) and South Africa (apartheid). In 1955, Nogueira described how Brazilians categorize difference based on appearance and color ("silvery brown" and "corn colored") which differed from the US emphasis on "biological ancestry" (one-drop of black "blood") in defining blackness. The biracial model (mutually exclusive categories of Black and/or white) has long shaped how race is thought about in the US (although this is changing). This perspective was institutionalized in the census and the collection of statistics on a number of social indicators. In Brazil, difference is rarely expressed as "white" or "Black." Color categories change with income, education, and context. For example, dark-skinned persons are more likely to be called "Black" (regardless of self-identification) if they are poor. Someone with the same pigmentation, but a higher income, is likely to be referred to as *moreno* (brown) leading to the expression "Money whitens."

In the 1950s, UNESCO sponsored an international research team to document Brazil's apparent success at achieving racial harmony. The results, however, showed a less favorable picture of Brazilian race relations. Rather than focusing on folklore, research undertaken by scholars at the "São Paulo School" in the 1950s and 1960s—Roger Bastide and Florestan Fernandes (1959), Fernando Henrique Cardoso (1962), and Octavio Ianni (1962, 1972, 1978)—analyzed class through "color," showing how this affected quality of life and opportunity in Brazil in significant ways. Although Degler suggested that the "mulatto escape hatch" (1971, p. 224) allowed lighter-skinned, "mixed" persons to achieve social and economic mobility, there was little empirical evidence to support this theory (Skidmore, 1983). Blacks were absent in politics, business, industry, law, and the military (Santos, 2005, p. 61). They had the highest rates of illiteracy, unemployment, poverty, and homicide (Hasenbalg, 1979; Silva, 1985). These studies effectively "put to rest" notions of a racial democracy (Fontaine, 1980, p. 129); however they have not eliminated the discursive power of racial harmony in shaping social relations.

During the Estado Novo (1937-45) and military dictatorship (1964-85), class, ethnic, and other solidarities were repressed as divisive and threatening to the state's nationalism project (Yúdice, 2003, p. 71; Andrews, 1991, p. 7; Azevedo, 1975). Those who described inequity as racially or ethnically based were criticized as "racists" and subversive (Andrews, 1991, p. 7). In the late 1970s, Abdias do Nascimento (1991), an Afro-Brazilian writer and politician, developed the notion of *Quilombismo* as a framework for interpreting and *responding to* the conditions of Afro-Brazilians. According to Nascimento, slavery's injustices did not end with abolition, but "persisted in multiple and complex ways" (Berliner, 2005, p. 588; Nascimento, 1978). *Quilombismo* encouraged the valorization of Afro-Brazilian culture and a rehistorization of benign descriptions of slavery popularized by social historican Gilberto Freyre in the 1930s (see Tannenbaum, 1946). Unilateral and aestheticized descriptions of plantation life, where everyone "knew their place," was challenged by evidence showing high mortality, runaways, rebellions, and revolts, discrediting the "common sense" ideology asserting racial harmony (Gramsci, 1971). The estimated 2,228 *quilombo* communities (descendants of fugitive slaves) in Brazil also attested to significant resistance to slavery.[13]

A number of scholars have critically examined how the state manipulates and suppresses racial and ethnic inequality by selecting and affirming "tolerable" folklore among those who are "poor in material goods but rich in spirit" (Yúdice, 2003, p. 112). African-influenced food, music, art, language, religion, architecture, dance, and sports are celebrated, but primarily as apolitical symbols of *national* patrimony. For example, *capoeira*, a previously *outlawed* martial arts/dance among Afro-Brazilians, has been recast as national patrimony.[14]

Since the *abertura*, there have been a number of political actions and policies initiated by Afro-Brazilians that have upset notions concerning the nation's racial harmony.[15] The vitriolic backlash to affirmative action for Blacks in federal, state and local institutions, and quotas in university admissions, have shown the divisiveness among mostly white elites and scholars, and Black activists. [16] Black-movement activists have encouraged "purification" of blackness by merging "mixed" categories of identification such as *mestiço*, *mulato*, *moreno*, and *pardo* into "Black," de-emphasizing a valued notion of whiteness (Oliveira e Oliveira 1974). In general, however, people are reluctant to identify as Black in a context where blackness is stigmatized (Nobles,

2000; Sansone, 2003). According to the 2000 census, a little over 6 per cent identified as Black.

A dark-skinned child asked me,

> Is it true what we see on TV about Blacks and whites in the States? That Black people live in one place and whites in another? If I show up there, will whites beat me up? We get along here; we don't have that kind of thing. Racism does not exist in Brazil, not like in the US. Here it is economic. There are lots of poor people, of all colors. If you went to Bahia you would see lots more Blacks, living well. The thing is, the poor in the United States live like the middle class in Brazil. Even the maids have cars. But it is true that we do not have a Black like Colin Powell.

The darker skinned kids I knew, all of them poor, felt they were constantly suspect for muggings, drug use, and rapes, akin to the expression in the United States "driving while Black" to describe the essentialized and criminal attitudes ascribed to Blacks. The majority of the trainees in my *capoeira* class were dark-skinned, low-income, young adults from the area. Although the majority of my neighbors were dark-skinned and poor as well, they warned me that *capoeira* is associated with the "Blacks," illicit drug use, and idle delinquents. Fofão, one of the many *guias* (tourist guides) in town, often spoke of the discrimination the Black guides, who are mistaken for thieves, faced.

> I know people think that Brazil does not have racism, but it is very strong here. It usually works this way. When you do not need something, then racism does not exist. When you need it, then you see it. For example, if you are at school and both you and your friend (who is not Black) get the same grade, okay. But then when you go for the job, the white kid will get it. Also, if you have things, like a car, etc., you tend to be respected more, just because you have these things. Usually when people talk about an educated Black person, people are

surprised, as if a Black person is not capable of that. You know, the police would harass me all the time, for nothing, thinking I was a street kid, but I wasn't. Just as a joke, you know, they took all my documents one time and told me I had to come for them at the police station. When I got there, the officer was not there, and they said they did not know when he would be back. So I had to wait days to get my documents back. Just the other day a cop took at a friend of mine; he was sniffing glue, and he just started kicking him, then took the glue and poured it on his head and body. The thing is, he could file a complaint, but he would never be safe. He would have to leave the area for fear of reprisal.

Mary: Do the police leave you alone when they know you, since many of the policemen live in the communities?

No. Only if you are a relative and even that is usually after the fact. "Oh, aren't you so and so's nephew? Sorry about that," meaning the kick, punch, or slap you got. The cops know the thieves. They wait for you to do a job, then go to your house and take everything. The police in Olinda are thieves. If you meet up with them at night, they will ask you for money. If you say you do not have any, wham! They hit you with the stick. It really doesn't matter if they are from the same bairro or favela. They learn, with the uniform, that they have power. They are told that. It has nothing to do with any internal power. Black cops are the worst. Overall, most of them are illiterate, and they hardly make two minimum salaries. No one really wants to be a cop, but it's a job. Sometimes the police beat people up for the fun of it.

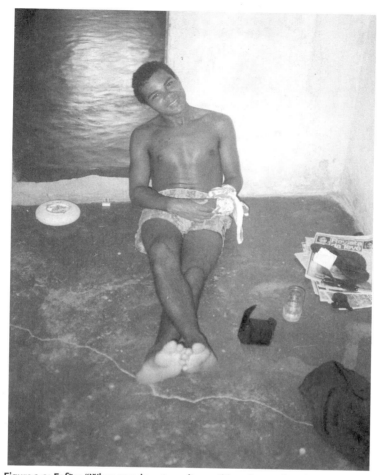

Figure 3.2: Fofão: "When you do not need something, then racism does not exist. When you need it, then you see it." Photo by Gigi.

Demiris, a three-year-old beggar, did not solicit as much attention and money because, according to her mother, "*ela é feia*" (she's ugly). "Look at her! She looks like a boy," her mother would lament. Demeris' pigmentation was darker than the rest of her siblings. She had short, kinky hair and was called Black, not *morena*, like her lighter-skinned older sister. Demiris would paint her mouth and cheeks with bright red lipstick and put on a dress in an attempt to look more "feminine" and attractive, although she resembled a clown or carnival player and most people just passed her by.

Figure 3.3: Demiris, 2000. Photo by author.

My housemate, Gigi, was an Afro-Brazilian female with nylon braid extensions. Women in the neighborhood repeatedly offered to "de-Africanize" her by straightening her hair, which would give her a "good" (whiter) appearance. Hair is a powerful symbol that reflects cultural norms, politics, and power. In a society dominated by white standards, "good" hair is straight. Black women with straight hair are seen as less aggressive and "ethnic" (Banks, 2000). Gigi felt that straightening her hair would indicate self-loathing, even though "good" hair would increase her chances of landing a job. I repeatedly witnessed her being turned down for jobs, mostly in the service industry, where the female employees were white or very light-skinned, and most of the patrons, white. She lamented, "There is no way I am going to be hired, because of my hair; I am too Black-looking. I am a descendant of slaves. Black women have always been serving in Brazil, since the days of slavery, when they breastfed white women's kids so that the white women's breasts would stay nice and pretty." Neighbors would ask if it was weird for me to live with a

Black woman, given the reputation for racism in the US. They assumed she was my maid. Why else would we be living together? Other girls in the neighborhood asked if they could become my maid too.

For a while Gigi dated a white, married man from the area. Gigi's mother, a light-skinned woman from the rural interior, admonished her to "not mess with a white man, because it will never work out. You should stay with men of your own color." Gigi's father was dark-skinned, and she was referred to as "your father's daughter." Of her mother's 22 births, Gigi was the darkest, and she claims, least loved because of it.

Figure 3.4: Gigi with her mother, 1994. Photo by author.

Her boyfriend commented that

> I would only consider having a serious relationship with women on a color scale above Gigi's color; any tone farther down is too black. Brazil is not racist like the US. Everyone here is equal, except I would not marry a Black, because I don't like the color. That's all it is. I just think that everyone should stick with their own color. I don't have a problem with Blacks. When people start with this kind of discussion [about Brazilian racism], I cut them off. I think it is meaningless.

Figure 3.5: Gigi during Carnival, 1995. Photo by author.

A CULTURE OF ZEBRAS

> People talk about Class A, B, C, but the poor are class
> Z, like a zebra, because they came out all wrong.
>
> —Ramos Melo

Some scholars have theorized that it is "culture" (the beliefs, values, way of life, etc.) among the poor that keep them trapped in cycles of poverty, rather than structural circumstances. This theory was popularized in 1966, when the North American anthropologist Oscar Lewis coined the term "subculture of poverty" to describe a number of traits

40

that he observed among the poor (fatalism, inability to defer gratification, low self-esteem) that were barriers to economic mobility (Lewis, 1966a,b). Despite this model being for the most part passé in anthropology, the "culture of poverty" concept continues to be a popular explanation for intergenerational destitution. Fifty years ago, in his seminal work *The Geography of Hunger* (1952), Brazilian geographer Josué de Castro critiqued the elitist perspective of blaming the poor for both creating and reproducing poverty, as it failed to differentiate what is *culturally shared* from what is *class-driven*. According to the culture of poverty model, the ubiquity of child labor among the poor reflects a distinct type of socialization (reproduction of culture) creating "little entrepreneurs" who get an early start on their inevitable future as unskilled, low-wage workers. This view not only naturalizes inequity, but fails to acknowledge that this "common sense" behavior is not an aspect of culture, but a response to material need (Rizzini, Rizzini, & Borges, 1998). It is important to tease apart structural conditions (unemployment, low wages, post-industrialization), cultural labels (work ethic), and a political economy shaped by paternalism, kin obligation, and labor niches for children, that shape poverty discourse. If child labor is an aspect of lower-class culture, the model would logically have to include crowded conditions, unemployment, and malnutrition as other aspects of that "culture." Confounding class with culture means the upper classes have *cultural* traditions that include living in high-rises with maids and sending their children to private schools. If child labor is seen as an aspect of *Brazilian* culture, why is the work that poor kids do unsuitable for middle- and upper-class children in Brazil, whose parents hire someone to do these tasks?

Development projects also tend to treat culture as an autonomous "variable" that can be inserted, removed, or re-engineered, rather than as a *relationship* (Fischer, 2003, p. 7). More than ever, neo-liberal economic policies and the decline of state welfare have reconfigured the role of "culture" as a "magic bullet" for development (Yúdice, 2003, p. 156; Edelman & Haugerud, 2005, p. 2). Culture is increasingly seen as a scaffold for weak schools, as a vehicle for solving racial tension, tackling problems such as crime and unemployment, reducing structural inequities, and enhancing one's well-being and self-esteem. I have often been asked to consult in the drafting and/or translation of grant proposals that seek funding for teaching "folklore" to low-income children, asserting that this raises their self-esteem and generates income. Brazilian Minister of Culture Gilberto Gil and the World Bank endorse culture as an "instrument for citizenship and social inclusion"[17] and the "driving force behind human development" (Ministry of Culture, 2006). Gil privileges economically marginal communities as those with the most "cultural assets."[18] For the last 10 years, army jeeps have taken tourists on a three-hour "pro-poor" tour to Rocinha, Brazil's largest favela for US$30.[19] Although groups may be instrumentally or strategically creating projects where "culture" is used as a development tool, it remains to be seen how effectively this fulfills the political goals of local agency, self-representation, and economic development.

NOTES

1. In 1919, the "Northeast" of Brazil was created as a separate geographical space from the "North" (Albuquerque, 1999). The Northeast includes nine states (Bahia, Pernambuco, and Ceará, and six smaller states: Alagoas, Maranhão, Paraíba, Piauí, Rio Grande do Norte, and Sergipe). It comprises 18.2 per cent of the nation's territory, 28 per cent of the country's population, and produces 14 per cent of the country's GNP.

2. *Caipira* comes from the Tupi word *caa-pir*, meaning lawn-cutter (Mugnaini, 2006).

3. The *abertura* refers to the gradual process of re-democratization and the development of a new Constitution in 1988.

4. *Coronels* were "anyone worthy of respect." They could be large landowners, businessmen, bankers, those with moral authority, and so on who were tied into an elite network of political, religious, and judicial authorities. Historically they are seen as controlling rural "fiefdoms" through these social networks (Domingos, 2004).

5. BBC. (2005, May 4). Brazil turns down US AIDS funds. Retrieved from <http://news.bbc.co.uk/1/hi/world/americas/4513805>.

6. Chico Mendes (Francisco Alves Mendes Folha) was a rubber tapper who fought for worker and environmental rights. He was assassinated in 1988.

7. According to the Electoral Code, article 299, "to give, offer, promise, solicit, or receive for oneself or another, to obtain ... votes is not accepted" and carries a penalty of up to four years in prison. See Caetano (2000, p. 264) cited in Goldani (2001) on payments for tubal ligations by politicians in Northeast Brazil. Brazil has a "culture of sterilization" (Potter, 1999, p. 729) and one of the highest rates of sterilization in all of Latin America. According to Family Health International (FHI), 40 per cent of women ages 15–49, who are married or in unions, have been sterilized. It is theorized that the high prevalence is due to limited access to other contraceptive methods. Studies show that the overwhelming majority of women are satisfied with their decision and do not regret it (FHI, 2004). Beginning in the late 1980s, feminist and Black women's movements (GELEDÉS, 1991) denounced the widespread use of sterilization as donor-directed, part of an international conspiracy to control reproduction among poor, non-white populations (Berquó, 1999).

8. DIEESE (Departamento Intersindical de Estatística e Estudos Sócio-Econômicos) Inter Trade Union Department of Statistics and Socio-Economic Studies provides a comparative, monthly accounting from 16 different cities in Brazil of the cost of a "basket" of 13 basic food staples, called the "basic food basket" (*cesta básica*). They also calculate how many hours someone earning the minimum wage will have to work in order to buy this basket. The basket takes into account regional differences in cost and includes, meat, milk, beans, rice, flour, potatoes, tomatoes, bread, coffee, banana, sugar, oil, and butter. The free baskets given out may substitute these items, or increase some and leave out others (2005).

9. According to Nancy Scheper-Hughes, caloric intake for adult male sugar cane cutters in Pernambuco (1500–1700) is less than those who interned at Buchenwald (1996a, p. 893).

10. There are 6.5 million women in the country who work as maids. 4.8 million do not have a *carteira assinada*, a signed work card, which entitles them to benefits. In the RMR, there are 103,000 women who work as maids. Sixty-seven thousand (65 per cent) work without a *carteira assinada* (Falcão 2006).

11. A 1939 law established the monthly minimum wage to cover the basic necessities of food, rent, clothing, transportation, and hygiene (Law no. 399, article 2).

12. Approximately 1 per cent of rural landowners in Brazil own 50 per cent of the land. It is estimated that 40 per cent of farmland is unused, or used only for cattle grazing. Since the 1960s, land reform has been seen as a crucial avenue for redistributing income and alleviating poverty. Since the mid-1980s, the *Movimento dos Trabalhadores Rurais Sem Terra* (Movement of Rural Landless workers—MST) has advocated for land reform through the redistribution of public land and fertile, unproductive private land to landless families, the development of cooperatives, and training, credit, and technological assistance for small farmers (of less than five hectares), rural workers, tenants, sharecroppers, and the urban poor. This is a highly contentious, regionally fractured, and dangerous form of activism, with over a thousand persons killed since the mid-1980s. The MST has faced difficulty organizing landless rural workers in the Northeast because their relationship to the land through their labor differs from those in the southern part of Brazil, where there was a stronger peasant tradition. In the sugar cane region of Pernambuco, rural workers prefer wage labor and paternalistic protection to ownership of "someone else's land" and "interference" by the overseers of land reform (Wolford, 2004, p. 147). Yet Aragão e Frota (1984) found that landless rural dwellers prefer working a piece of land, which provides a minimal amount of food, to dependence on low wages as rural workers that barely covers subsistence.

13. The 1988 Constitution, article 68, supports the petitioning for land titles based on being a descendant of slaves in quilombos.

14. *Capoeira* is now practiced and taught by peoples of all races, ethnicities and classes. Although this raises questions about its role as a national/ Brazilian versus ethnic-cultural heritage, there is no denying the symbolic and economic capital that *capoeira* now has worldwide. People come from all over the world to Brazil to participate in *capoeira* groups. It is taught in day care centers, health clubs, and schools. *Capoeiristas* are hired to work on cruise ships and tourist sites around the world. As a trainer, *capoeira* provides opportunities for income and travel not otherwise available for lower income persons.

15. The International Covenant on Economic, Social and Cultural Rights (CESCR), and the International Covenant on Civil and Political Rights (CCPR), outlined in 1966, were signed by Brazil in 1992. These documents state that all peoples have the right to determine and pursue their economic, social, and cultural development.

16. See Maio and Santos (2005) for an insightful analysis of the process of weeding out "fake" Blacks from the University of Brasilia's affirmative action program. A tribunal of "experts" developed a "scientific" (objective) measure of "Blackness" to determine merit by evaluating photos of candidates to assess their "African" traits and interviewing candidates to determine if they were psychologically and socially "Black." This practice generated significant debate, focusing on the asymmetric use of experts, rather than self-ascription, to determine identity. The implementation of an affirmative action program in universities is a hotly debated topic, and has been referred to as "racist, commanded by the United States and exported to the periphery by the Ford Foundation" (Andrade, 2006).

17. Brazil wants culture as a basic human right. *Brazzil Magazine*. (2004, August 27). Retrieved from <http://www.brazzil.com>.

18. Gil, Gilberto. (2005, February 21). Presentation at Columbia University, School of International Affairs.

19. Brazil's insertion in this "market for suffering" (Kleinman, Das, & Lock, 1997, p. xi) or "black spot" tourism" (Rojek, 1993, p. 136) has been equated with the rubbernecker's experience of passing by and gazing at someone else's tragedy (Cole, 1999, p. 114). Ignatieff has called it a form of tourism for "voyeurs of the suffering of others, tourists amidst landscapes of anguish" (1998, pp. 10–11).

CHAPTER FOUR
OLINDA

Figure 4.1: Olinda. Photo by author.

Olinda is a located on the Atlantic Ocean, 6 kilometers north of Recife. The area was "given" to Duarte Coelho Pereira by the Portuguese King John III in 1534 as one of the many *capitanias* or areas to be developed and administered by a wealthy entrepreneur on behalf of the king. Through the exportation first of brazilwood (based on the labor of enslaved Indians), then sugar cane (based on the labor of enslaved Africans), the colony flourished. In 1630 the Dutch invaded Pernambuco. For 25 years, they dominated a huge expanse from what is today Sergipe to Ceará. The capital was transferred to Recife (because it resembled Amsterdam) and Olinda was razed. Recife developed into an active port and a center of trade and culture. Today Olinda has a population of almost 368,000 and is the third-largest city in Pernambuco. In 1982, it was designated a world heritage city by UNESCO, and in 2005 was awarded the title "Capital of Culture" in all of Brazil.

Figure 4.2: Carnival in Olinda. Photo by author.

Olinda is noted for its sixteenth- and seventeenth-century ornate churches, monasteries, and colonial buildings and attracts artists, musicians, and numerous tourists to the area. *Carnaval*, the holiday season prior to Lent, is the peak tourist season in Olinda. About 1,000–2,000 jobs are generated during this time, both legal and illegal, in restaurants and bars, the souvenir trade (which is the main outlet for local craft producers), the letting of houses in the old city, and for taxi drivers and tourist guides.

Figure 4.3: Carnival in Olinda. Photo by author.

The city government is the largest employer, with over 6,000 employees. The *povo*[1] chronically complain that it is bloated and ineffective. Government positions (federal, state, and municipal) are coveted because they are viewed as sinecures where someone gets paid for doing little or no work. Government employees are referred to as *maharajahs* because they live like kings without having to labor. One morning I was conducting an interview with a municipal employee in her office in the town hall, when all of a sudden we heard the chants of a crowd approaching City Hall. "What's going on?" I asked. "Oh, don't mind that. It's a just a protest. They'll probably come up here, but they won't bother us." Within five minutes they had entered the second floor of the city hall, and were next to us shouting and chanting. She continued to speak to me as if they were not there, and I strained to hear her barely audible voice against the 100 or so protestors who were asking to speak to the mayor about unfulfilled promises to generate jobs. One of the protesters was shouting, "The mayor is corrupt, a thief, has promised to help us, has not done anything! I want him to eat a carrot from my ass, and I want to put a bomb in his car!"

Although much of Olinda is located on the coast, the local, public beach is frequented for the most part by those who cannot afford to go anywhere else. It is popularly called the *Praia do Cocô* (poop beach). Raw sewage is visibly pumped into the water, and although advised not to swim in it, most locals do. The result is itchy rashes, colds, and other skin afflictions.

Figure 4.4: Feast of St. Peter, patron saint of fishermen, June 29. Photo by author.

Close by is the *Inferninho* (little hell) located inside the Ilha do Maruim, a local favela. On Sundays local girls and women dance and drink with the men, and rent out small rooms in the back for an hour or so for R$22[2] (R$20 for the girl and R$2 for rent of the room). At the same time across the street a Bible study class is held, where a pastor sets up a few chairs for a skimpy audience of mostly elderly women. The Ilha, as it is called locally, also borders the Praia del Cifre, popular with local surfers.[3] The garbage that the tide brings to its shores provides a telling glimpse of urban waste. One day a bloated, dismembered head washed ashore.

FAVELAS

Figure 4.5: House in favela. Photo by Tônio.

Favelas are a glaring example of the "hierarchy of place" (Harvey, 1989). They are important sites for examining social relations, citizenship, and human rights. My students in the US often ask me why people do not just leave and move to another location, or why they come to certain favelas in the first place.

People enter and leave particular favelas for different reasons. Some are newcomers to the city from the "interior" (popularly referred to as any area outside the urban center). Others circulate between different favelas based on availability of land and proximity to work and family. Shifts in land use are key factors in determining stability and longevity. Land that appears abandoned or unproductive does not guarantee land ownership to squatters, nor does it mean that owners (including the state) will not at some point demand all squatters be removed or relocated for development projects.

Favelas are considered squatter settlements and therefore residents do not own the land. However residents sell their homes all the time. Real estate speculators also "claim" plots, and then sell them. Changing labor conditions, such as the opening of a factory that requires construction workers, may bring families into a nearby favela. Violence, particularly retaliation for killings, is a key factor in movement in and out of favelas. Changes in the household, such as the birth of a child or the separation of a couple, may force relocation. Some families I knew had lived in the same favela for three generations.

Thirty years ago, the term favela was defined by the *Instituto Brasileiro de Geografía e Estastística* (IBGE, Brazilian Institute of Geography and Statistics) as: (a) a minimum number of 51 buildings grouped together; (b) a predominance of huts and barracks of a typical rustic appearance, usually made of planks and galvanized sheets or similar material; (c) unlicensed and uninspected buildings on lands of third parties or unknown owners; (d) not included in the general network of sewerage, running water, lighting, and telephones; (e) a non-urbanized area, lacking proper division into streets, numbering, feeing, or rating system (Wolf & Hansen, 1972, p. 162). However, favelas, like any community, are heterogeneous in terms of their size, density, location, infrastructure, use of space, movement in and out of the community, access to resources, and political organization. The history of the community (why it is located where it is, and how it has grown), laws and policies concerning land use, levels of violence, segregation, and the involvement of NGOs, academics, and other professional mediators in the community mean that the social, political, and historical landscape is always shifting.

Figure 4.6: After the rain. Photo by Tônio.

The term favela was originally used by Euclides da Cunha in *Os Sertões* (Rebellion in the Backlands) in 1902. He was a Brazilian engineer and sociologist who wrote an account of the military destruction of Canudos, Bahia, a utopian community (1893-97) led by Antônio Conselheiro, a messianic leader who for 20 years in the late nineteenth century traveled the backlands of Brazil. The author described both the scrub and the mountain where followers of Conselheiro were located as favela. Veterans of the Canudos War (1897) later built houses in Rio de Janeiro that they named *Favela Mountain*. The term later referred to any shantytown settlement. Favelas are also referred to as *invações* (invasions), referring to the illegal occupation of land.

Brazil is a land of contrasts, and nowhere is this more apparent than in the juxtaposition of the ornate historic district of Olinda (Cidade Alta), with its winding streets, sixteenth-century churches, old fountains, seminaries, and schools, and the 60 favelas found in the rest of the city. Approximately 60 per cent of the population lives in favelas and low-income neighborhoods. Only 300 meters from the cobbled streets and large homes behind high gates, barbed wire, and charred glass are some of the most poor and violent zones in Olinda, where the majority of working children live. Both their playground and their workplace are "public," in contrast to upper-class children who remain primarily within the confines of the apartment building or house. These houses are often surrounded by a cement wall topped with broken glass to prevent entry. Some have private security guards as well.

Figure 4.7: My favela. Photo by Edna.

Plots of land and houses are small in favelas. The average dwelling ranges from 15 to 50 square meters. There is little space for storage, let alone large families. Many are inaccessible to cars and most people travel by foot or bicycle. Some favelas in Olinda are adjacent to marshland or mangrove swamps, such as V8, a 50-year-old favela and the adjacent V9. When there are heavy rains, water, sewage, and mud fill the houses of the over 2,000 families living there. Leptospriosis (a disease acquired through the contaminated urine of rats), and tuberculosis are chronic afflictions. According to Dona Bete, "Here there is no security. Babies die, even the rats die."[4]

People earn a living through petty trading, usually from roadside stalls or street markets—selling secondhand goods, small items of cooked food, fruit, drinks, cosmetics, and clothes. Garlic, for example, will be broken up and sold for 10 centavos a clove. Every available economic niche is capitalized on, although competition is intense and limited by the low purchasing power of the community. In other words, selling to each other is not very profitable, and higher-income consumers in general do not enter favelas. The purchase of illicit drugs for members of the upper classes is usually done by an *avião* (airplane), who is usually a small-time dealer.

Favela residents have different jobs, education, and income levels. The majority of my informants lived in V8 and V9, or in one-room *cortiços* (called "beehives," where the bathroom and water are shared with other residents). One of the entrances is off a major access road named "President Kennedy." A few houses at the entrance are owned by long-term residents and constructed from brick and cement. Others are constructed from wood, or a combination of paper and wood. Some have iron grills covering windows, backyard gardens with mango trees, caged birds, and two floors. There are a few cars, and small shops where canned goods, *cachaça* (a cheap, powerful rum made from sugar cane), and other household items are sold, and domestic appliances are repaired and sold. A sinewy river of small paths leads deeper into the favela.

Figure 4.8: V8. Photo by Dalva.

The more recent arrivals live deeper in the favela and have homes "in progress": only three walls, no doors, and so forth. Tile roofs are expensive, so most homes have tin roofs. Tiled floors are rare; most have cement or dirt floors. A few homes have built latrines, but many construct makeshift outhouses out of wooden slats or large palms. Clothes substitute as sheets, electricity is "stolen" (spliced wires from those who have electricity) and woven through various homes. Water is hauled from a privately owned pipe for which they pay a small fee. The kids begin to line up at dawn, fetching water with old gas and oil cans, adroitly balancing the cans, which are often the same size as they are, on their heads.

Figure 4.9: Washing dishes. Photo by Tônio.

Open drains and the "Malaria Canal" emit a year-round wretched stench. Domestic hardware is found in even the poorest homes, although it is rarely purchased. Blenders, gas stoves, refrigerators, televisions, and stereos are salvaged and repaired by residents. Certain jobs, for example women who work as maids, increase access to hardware that their employers throw away. Those without stoves (or who run out of gas) cook with kerosene-soaked cotton atop a bottle.

Figure 4.10: Living room. Photo by Rosie.

In the US, it is generally considered "healthy" for children to have their own bedroom, or share a bedroom with another sibling. Privacy is normal and expected. In the favelas, privacy is an aberration. Dwellings are crowded and indoor space is scarce. Houses are close together, windows are low, and anyone passing by can look in. Domestic arguments can be overheard by everyone.

Reports in the media tend to highlight the violence in favelas. In November 1994, the army was authorized to enter some favelas in Rio as a response to the increasing power and control of drug traffickers. Dramatic shots of tanks and machine guns amidst the crumbling shacks of the favelas were broadcast across the country. The "ordinary citizen" in Rio approved the move, but some local residents thought the intervention ineffective and comical, especially given the number of police involved in drug trafficking. Guns could be purchased on the street for about US$180, and ammunition for about US$10–$15. A letter from an anonymous *favelado* was published in the local newspaper, *Jornal do Commercio*, and posted on the walls of local bars. The letter read as follows:

> I am the beginning of a new era. Don't you understand that I am a sign? You have turned away for decades. You hate me because I am ugly, dirty, poor. You have always removed me from your conscience, and now you will remove me with arms. Today, I am the beginning of your social conscience. The diagnosis has always been the same: migration (of unskilled workers) from the rural areas, a need for increase in the infrastructure, etc. etc. But the solution never came. No one, ever, has ever looked at favelas, because we don't exist; when the rats attack us at night, we don't exist. When we die of hunger, from the rain, we are only good photos for the papers (they sell a lot), and we provoke anguish among sensitive intellectuals ... but now you are all in panic because we are armed, we are not just a moral problem. We have AR-15s, AK-47s, Uzis ... we are united ... we are the "bad" and you the "good" citizen. You don't know death; for you death is a Christian drama, for us a daily occurrence. You think we are a problem for you? You are a problem for us! Why don't the armed forces get those who sell us arms and live in Ipanema? The death of a poor person is not tragic. The armed forces are just dying to act, to justify their existence; they have something to do now besides play basketball at the headquarters. They like action (it must be hard living without a war, without a dictatorship). We also like the arms we see in the films like *Rambo*. And I am just a hors-d'oeuvre for the grand banquet to come. It is going to be the era of insolvable problems. Haiti is going to be here, yes. The solution will come after much death, after mouths are filled with ants, after you know the concrete fact of rats, instead of the sweet life of the

bureaucrat and politician. Why not try a more rapid
solution? A bomb, perhaps, in each favela ... then all
the area can be urbanized and sold.[5]

There is significant illicit drug consumption and distribution in
Olinda, with sporadic shootouts between police and drug dealers, as well
as "revenge" killings. One resident described her life in V9 as follows:
"When we are all in the house together it is total chaos. Listening on the
radio is horrible because you do not know what anyone looks like, or
who is saying what. At least with a television you can send the kids to sit
in front of it, like a baby sitter. Here you cannot talk with the neighbors.
There is nothing else to do here." Everyone I met living in a favela was
desperate to leave. "I would buy a house far from here, and take nothing, absolutely nothing, that would remind me I had ever lived here."
Although they acknowledged some solidarity, pooling, borrowing, and
sharing of resources, suspicion and lack of trust were chronic. "I say
nothing to anyone. I don't talk to anyone." When I would ask who they
depend on, a common response was "No one. When people see you are
doing well, they are jealous, not happy for you." One resident reported
angrily:

> All that stuff Nega tells you about having had such a
> hard time is bullshit. Just pass by her house and see
> what she's got. Go ahead! Her kids don't have to beg.
> They spend it all on clothes. She is even raising pigs,
> and the smell is horrible, in my house all day. It isn't
> good for my kids to be breathing this. People think you
> are giving us stuff and they are jealous. They come over
> after you leave to see.

Residents insisted that there was little cooperation and reciprocity,
that "everyone is out for themselves." I was constantly warned against as-
sociating with families who were *não presta* (good for nothings). "Don't
give a stove to that family. The father spends all their money on marijuana." Ten-year-old Pedro told me, "You should not give money to kids
who don't need it. If you don't believe me, look in her purse," and he
grabbed Rosie's purse and opened it.

See what I mean? Look at this! Ten *reais*. She doesn't
need the money. She has money. Her mother washes
clothes. If I had 10 *reais*, I wouldn't be here on the
street. I'd stay away for a few days. Rosie buys clothes.
She shows off. I have nothing, not even sheets. They
don't share anything. I don't really give a damn about
money. If I have it, okay. If you need it, I'll give to you.
If I don't have it, well, then I'll go hungry.

Communities are groups of people who identify themselves with a
place or places in terms of notions of commonality, shared values, experiences, histories, or solidarity in a particular context (Lovell, 1998; Platt,
1996). I observed numerous instances of "community" that countered
the above statements about suspicion and isolation. People joked with
each other and shared food, child care, and clothing. They communally
watched TV, especially the nightly soap operas. They ran errands for each
other and helped to purchase coffins or pay for other funeral expenses.
When Vera's boyfriend beat up her four-year-old daughter, Vera asked
two male friends to beat up the boyfriend. I observed a vibrant community of people working, talking, praying, cooking, drinking, rocking
babies, creating and playing music, dancing, and grooming each other.
Other ethnographic studies have shown the prevalence of close-knit families, class and political allegiances, and strong social networks in poor
communities. In her study of a Mexican shantytown, Larissa Lomnitz
(1988) noted the nature and extent of information, training and job assistance, loans, services, and other support that community members
share. Carol Stack (1974) documented the extent of cooperative networks
among low-income, urban African-Americans in "The Flats," as did a
study of a favela in Rio de Janeiro by Perlman (1976).

Nonetheless, the sentiments expressed by informants are more akin to
those found by Pearse in his 1961 study of a favela in Rio de Janeiro. The
women he interviewed insisted that trust with neighbors was absent, that
they do not visit others' homes, and prohibit their children from doing so
as well. They concurred with Maria de Jesus' description of favela life: the
least friendly and cooperative place is the favela. Although pooling, borrowing, and sharing of resources are present, it is shadowed by suspicion
and scarcity (Jesus, 1962).

NOTES

1. *Povo* (people) refers to the impoverished and mostly non-white members of the lower classes. Although the term has taken on various meanings (proletarians, soul of national identity), I use the term as my informants do: those who are not the privileged in society, but who make privilege possible.

2. Brazilian currency is measured in reais.

3. A shark attack in June 2006 killed a local surfer. Since 1992, there have been 49 shark attacks in Pernambuco, 18 fatal (Comitê de Monitoramento de Incidentes com Tubarões, CEMIT).

4. In June 2006, a major urban development project began in V8 and V9, with funding from the World Bank and state and local governments. The redevelopment project includes draining and enlarging the "Malaria Canal," paving streets, providing access to sewage and water systems, and building new homes. Residents are scrambling to "upgrade" their homes, as they will receive indemnity payments to leave.

5. *Journal do Commercio.* (1994, November 2). Translation mine.

CHAPTER FIVE
WORK AND SCHOOL IN URBAN BRAZIL

Figure 5.1: Hard at work. Photo by Ana.

> The best thing that has ever happened to me is
> to become an adult and manage my own life.
>   —Jorge, age 12

In this next chapter, I discuss some of the particular labor niches children occupy within the context of their communities. Many girls work as domestics, while boys begin work early as tour guides. Domestic work in the home is unremunerated and seen as "normal" for females, and frees adults to work both inside and outside the home. Although they often spoke of themselves as the "head of the household," in practice there is little if any increase in autonomy, power, and decision making associated with children's earnings.

WORKING ONE'S WAY INTO ADULTHOOD

Pernambuco ranks third in its percentage of child laborers in the country. About half of all children between 10 and 18 contribute in some way to household income. It is assumed that child labor is most prevalent in households in which wage earning adult males are "absent," (female-headed households or matrifocal families).[1] However, a study conducted by the *Departamento Intersindical de Estatística e Estudos Sócio-Econômicos* (DIEESE) in 1995–96 with 1,500 working children in six cities showed that the majority had two working parents. Without more in-depth information on income, resources, and the economic niches available to children, there is no simple correlation between children working and family form.

In Olinda, children's work parallels that of adults in the informal sector. Both can be seen in the lowest paid and least stable jobs. For those under age 14, work is exclusively in the informal sector. This includes street vending, such as selling newspapers, and inexpensive household items and food. Children also shine shoes; wash and guard cars; prepare food (including working in makeshift, backyard chicken-processing "plants"), wash dishes and clean restaurants and bars; work as shop assistants; collect fares on *kombis* (privately operated vans); work as domestics; and scavenge for food and recyclables.

Figure 5.2: Female *catador* with *gancho*. Source: *Marinézia Gomez, Força e Solidão* (2002).

Approximately 45,000 children work in *lixões* (garbage dumps) in Brazil. In Olinda, the dump is located in Aguazinha, a few kilometers from the city center. The city produces approximately 700 tons of trash per day. In 1994, about 200 people lived in the *lixão* and depended on urban residue to survive (the number has since increased to 350). Non-residents also scavenge for recyclables such as paper, plastic, glass, wood, rubber, iron, aluminum, zinc, bronze, copper, lead, cans, newspapers, magazines, bones, and rags.

The *lixão* is located off the main road. The skyline is shaped by mountains of refuse and swirling vultures. If the garbage trucks have recently come in, the piles of refuse are dotted with persons sifting through it with an iron prod.

Figure 5.3: Arrival of truck. Source: *Jornal do Commercio* (1995, 12 March), p. 9.

Mud, the fetid smell from the mound of garbage, and large, biting flies dominate the environment. Tuberculosis, leptospirosis,[2] toxic substances, and broken glass further jeopardize health. The *lixão* is also a famous dumping ground for bodies.

The children in the *lixão* would talk about *"quando eu caí no lixão,"* literally, "when I fell into the garbage," to describe their move to the dump. They are ashamed to tell people where they live: "People think we are filthy.... Kids hold their noses when we walk by. Kids don't want to play with us, because they think our toys are from the garbage. It is impossible to clean the filth from the trash sometimes." Many have come from other favelas, having been displaced by urban development projects, or they move to the dump in order to get the "first choice" on materials when the trucks come in, what they call the "filet" of trash.[3]

Families live in makeshift shacks surrounded by scavenged, categorized trash (plastic bottles, glass, paper, etc.). Most shacks house from three to eight people. Houses have been constructed out of a combination of wood planks, plastic, mud, and canvas. Inside the homes are a variety of scavenged items: plates, spoons, glass jars, wood for fire. A number of homes have pets, kittens and puppies, tied to strings and ropes so they will not run away. One day I asked a kid the name of a listless little puppy tied to a chair. He went over to the puppy, then noted, "Oh, he's dead," and threw it on top of the garbage mound.

When the trucks come in, all family members head out to scavenge for recyclable material and discarded food. "The difficulty is that all of it is mixed together," one said, as he separated food from paper, cans, glass, and plastic, "with sanitary napkins and used toilet paper." Paper is the most valuable material. Cans and glass can also be sold, but glass is extremely difficult to handle. Some families can earn up to three minimum salaries, but one minimum salary is the average and scavenging is usually supplemented with other types of work. Prices for materials are set by the recycling plant. Although plant prices vary, it is almost impossible to spend time searching for better prices, since moving goods around town is very labor intensive, even with a cart. José, aged 12, said:

> If only the prices would go up, my situation would get a lot better. You have to have the experience to know what to separate and be able to utilize and sell. You have to know how to clean, weigh, and classify. The trucks begin arriving at 4:00 a.m. to unload the trash.... This

idea of being good, of giving to others, does not exist. Here, no one is friends with anyone. Like snakes eating snakes. You have to claim things swiftly; otherwise, someone else will claim it as their own. Then you have to clean it, because if not the flies will be all over.

In December 2003, the partner of one of the kids I had first interviewed in 1994 was killed in a dispute involving ownership of a plastic bag filled with trash. She had moved to the dump from her mother's house in a nearby favela, which she felt was symbolic of her social and economic ascension. Being able to establish a separate household with a baby and partner is out of reach for most couples. In addition, at age 20 and with a child of her own, she had become more of a domestic liability than an asset. Her meager earnings as a maid (one minimum salary for working 11 hours per day/6 days per week) were now being redirected to her own child and partner. After her partner's murder (she and her baby were also threatened, since she had seen the face of the assailant), she was forced to leave the dump, with nowhere to go. Although she lived in the horrendous conditions described above, she felt she had some autonomy, that the income was stable if you hustled, and she was able to live with the father of her baby. When I saw her again, she was eking out a living here and there with her baby until she could find somewhere in the "interior" to live and escape the favelas.[4]

Sometimes *lixão* owners help residents with medical and other exigencies, with an understanding that they "reciprocate" by taking scavenged materials to their friend's recycling centers. The owner said he was wary about providing any kind of services, such as water, or about giving people gloves to use, because he was afraid it would be an incentive for others to move there. In 1996, the city spent a day providing free immunizations for *catadores*, to protect them from occupational hazards. Ironically, they would not give out boots or gloves because they said the *catadores* would sell them.

Children described their work as scavengers as superior to begging: "It is better to pick garbage than steal or beg. If I steal, I might be arrested. If I begged, I would never know how much I could earn. Any kind of work is better than being a bum. Besides, you get used to this."

BEGGARS

If I don't work, my family will go hungry. I can take it. It is my fate.

—Dalva, age 12

Whether parading a blind father or baring a scar for profit, the role of mendicant is one of the few regular income-earning options for children, regardless of sex. Compassion stands in inverse relationship to age; the younger the child, the more sympathy and money they receive. Guiding a blind adult or carrying a baby also enhances pity. Children would "borrow" infants from neighbors all the time.

Prime locations for begging are the tourist district of the Cidade Alta and the numerous bars and restaurants along the coast. They head out to the main tourist district at about 8:00 a.m., ready for the tourist buses that begin to arrive at about 10:00 a.m. They hang around the food stalls, which annoys the vendors. Tourists frequently offer food, but the kids prefer money. "I just want the money. It's easier to divide than food. That way we can buy what we want, and still come home with some money. When there's nothing to eat, my mother sends us out to beg. My father will kill us if we don't go out and bring something home." One day they take an entrepreneurial approach and combine what they earn and buy candy to sell at a profit. These ventures were rarely profitable because inevitably they ate more than they sold. On a good day, they make about 20 reais for a 12-hour day. According to the kids, most of their earnings go to their mothers. The kids usually stay until the tourists leave, sometimes hanging around the bars until dawn, but this does not assure them any additional income.

One day the kids asked if they could use my small, hand-held tape recorder to interview parishioners as they exited an early morning mass. They also interviewed each other, using Likert-scale questioning, about how the threat of physical abuse is an "incentive" to work.[5] "Do you get beaten a lot or a little if you come home with no money?" They were experts at targeting middle-aged women exiting the church. Rosie, aged 10, would put her arm around the women and walk with them, offering sympathy. "*Sim, senhora*, I know life is very hard." Camila would put on a sad face, and tug on the sleeves and skirts of parishioners exiting the church. At age 4, she was an expert at rendering pitiful expressions that included pouting with her lower lip and sticking out her stomach. Her uniform was a large, white, flamenco-style skirt that revealed both her protruding stomach and bottom.

The work they do is dangerous. One day I sat across the street and waited for Camila to return from a house where she had approached the gate to solicit food and/or money. The house was located on the hilltop of the historic district, with a view of the sea. The family had a reputation for sitting in the front parlor with the windows open while they listened to Vivaldi. The macabre incongruity to this scene occurred when their private security guard released their dog on Camila after she knocked on the gate. In a pre-emptive strike, the guard assessed that Camila was part of a gang that was using her as a front for a robbery, assault, or kidnapping. He let the dog loose, who promptly took a significant piece of flesh from her leg. The family apologized for the mishap, and gave her the equivalent of US$10 for medication. She gave the money to her mother, who used it for food.

Figure 5.4: Camila, 2001. Photo by Edna.

There was little evidence of any type of fixed income or consistent avail-ability of food. Although some kids could earn between half and one mini-mum wage per month, there was little correlation between hours worked and earnings. For example, Niña made 30 reais one week, giving 20 to her mother. With that, her mother bought tomatoes, onions, *farinha* (dried, grated manioc flour), coffee, and cigarettes, totaling R$13, leaving R$7 left over for eight people. The following week they sold two chickens for R$2 each, and bought food that lasted one day. The following day there was no food. The next week, the combined earnings of three children equaled R$35. I predicted that the money would be used for food, but instead their money bought lipsticks to resell for a profit and sheets for the bed, and paid a neighbor for damages incurred when her daughter slashed their couch.

Children also age out of particular ways to earn money. One day I was hanging around Dalva's house with her, her siblings, and her mother. Dalva came into the house from outside, where she had just taken a bath. Her mother began to tease her about her budding breasts, at the same time adding a rejoinder: "My goodness Dalva, cover your breasts! Don't you have any shame?" They made frequent comments about each other's bodies, teasing the baby about the size of his penis and pulling on it, or commenting on the size of neighborhood girls' behinds and breasts. Dalva's mother sighs and says to me, "She's becoming a *moça* now. I have to take her off the street and keep her home with me. Maybe I can get her a job working as a maid. People will look at her differently now." Then some women from the neighborhood came in, and began to comment: "Look at her. She's a *moça* now. She should not be on the street anymore. It's dangerous." Despite her mother's and the neighbors' lamentations, Dalva throws her head back and laughs, grabs her breasts, and dances a little samba to show off her growing body. She later tells me,

> I am so miserable. All I do is work. Did you know that today is my 12th birthday? What do I want? The thing I want the most is go get out of this miserable favela, but I have to help my mother. I have to go out again today and get together some money for tomorrow's break-fast. I am desperate to get out of this favela. The last time it rained, the water came up to here (the bed) and this place is filled with rats.

Her father walks in and she stops talking. He sees me, and leaves. "You know, he comes home, and if there is not a pan on the fire, you get beat.... Heh; you took all those pictures of the baby. How 'bout some pictures of me?" She whisks inside and emerges in a skimpy blue *fio dental*,[6] grabs my sunglasses, and poses. As I shoot the pictures, a local gang, with their pit bulls, ask me to photograph them as they stand tall and defiant.

Figure 5.5: Dalva, 1994: "All I do is work." Photo by author.

Regardless of her work and responsibilities, Dalva seemed to have little authority or rights (although this was changing). It was unclear to me what "rites of passage," social markers, or milestones would mark her transition to adulthood. In some societies, it is age, marriage, or child-birth. In others, it is menarche, leaving school, or a series of age-related acts that incrementally reflect adult rights, responsibilities, and obliga-tions. In the US, it may be financial independence from parents, vot-ing, or serving in the military. Gender and class also influence the social transition to adulthood. For many young Latin-American females, the *festa de quinze anos* or "coming out" party for 15-year-old girls is a public ritual that indicates a girl's transition to being a young woman. Those with resources spend a considerable sum to provide a party that at times appears more elaborate than a wedding. In turn, the celebrant receives gifts and money. Halfway through the evening, the celebrant changes from her "normal" party clothes to a white dress that resembles a bridal gown. Theoretically, the girl dressed as a bride is still a *moça* (meaning "girl" but also "virgin"). A *mulher* (woman) can also mean "knowing woman," one that has already had sexual intercourse. After dancing first with her father, the celebrant is presented or given by him to local young men, with whom she dances individually. Her new status theoretically includes restrictions on interaction between herself and unrelated adult men, which could result in pregnancy and raise issues about paternity, inheritance, and property transfers. Those without the means either go into great debt or do not provide such costly celebrations. None of the girls I knew had such a party given on their behalf. Among the lower classes, legally binding unions are less common and inheritance and property are frequently unavailable.

The comments by Dalva's mother about her budding breasts indicate both a physical shift to maturity and a probable economic shift in the household. Ideally, a "good," decent *moça* does not run the streets. Practically though, these gender norms would significantly curtail household earnings. Although the danger of assault, robbery, and so on have always existed, Dalva's sexualized status increases the possibility of pregnancy, which would redirect her earnings toward her own offspring.[7] Her mother frames this dilemma by saying, "Dalva does not want to work anymore," meaning Dalva is gradually keeping more of her earnings for herself. One day she purchased a pair of used high-heeled shoes and a wallet that had spaces for paper money and credit cards. Her mother began complaining that less money was ending up in her hands.

According to Dalva, she started to have "more of a say in things," undermining her mother's authority and decision making concerning how money was spent. A few months later, she announced, "My life is better now. No one tampers with my stuff." I watched as she ordered all the neighbors out of the house one day during an argument, stating with authority, "They have no right to stay since they speak badly about us." She was becoming increasingly more bold, confident, and independent. Her early and consistent support of her family had forced her to navigate the world beyond her home for years. Her mother, on the other hand, felt paralyzed when she had to deal with the bureaucracy of the town hall and local health clinic. She rarely ventured beyond the entrance to the favela. One day Dalva hopped on a bus to the interior, not returning for two weeks. She told me she was "tired and needed a break from everything."

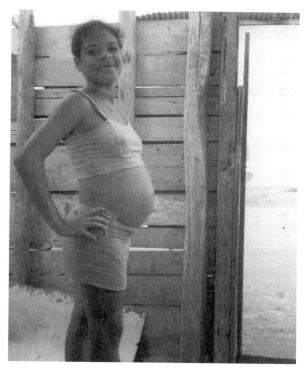

Figure 5.6: Dalva, 1999. Photo by Rosie.

In general, the younger in age they are, they less they keep for themselves. Kids would always say, "It goes to my mother." By age nine, sometimes before, most of the kids were expected to contribute economically to the household. However, their earnings did not seem to provide them with any special status or increased access to resources, although their work is "valued" because they earn cash, can access food, and create possibly lucrative connections with tourists and foreigners like me. Although they are reluctant to admit it, many parents were unsatisfied with their children's earnings (Folbre, 1986). Bete would complain that the money her son earned selling newspapers was insufficient. "It doesn't help much. He doesn't have to pay rent here, you know," and she often thought he lied about his earnings in order to keep more for himself.

Figure 5.7: Dalva with her baby (*center*). Photo by Edna.

Although the kids referred to themselves as "heads of the household," in practice there appeared to be little increase in autonomy, power, or decision making. Food was given for good behavior and withheld as punishment, and more and better food was systematically directed toward adult males. As they aged, the kids would also "eat like adults," putting additional strain on food resources. Differential food allocation is common in settings of chronic scarcity.[8] "We get some money, and buy some food. If no money, no food. Food is given to my father first, and then the rest divided among us," said Dalva. A prize job is one where the employer provides lunch, the biggest meal of the day, but these are rare. Most of the maids had their meals discounted from their pay. Meat, gas for cooking, and school supplies are all luxury items. Inexpensive and high-protein foods such as beans were forfeited because they required so much gas or kerosene to prepare. One mother told me in a rage,

> The people who donate this stuff (food) think we're stupid. These beans are no good. They're old and hard, and I have to cook them forever. I have to waste the little kerosene I have [she cooked them on top of a bottle stuffed with cotton and kerosene]. You know,

> we might be poor, but I don't want someone else's
> leftovers, the stuff other people throw away. The poor
> quality beans, flour, clothes, and stuff that rots. The
> donated flour is bad, and they know that, but we are
> supposed to use it anyway. This is stuff you would not
> give to a dog. We are supposed to be happy with this?
> So I throw them away.

A new baby brought an additional mouth to feed, and illness meant the loss of earnings and the expense of medication. Any loss of earnings brought adjustments in consumption. Kids were encouraged to find others to feed them, which had the effect of reducing their domestic consumption.[9] On a good day, people would buy them soft drinks, cookies, and sandwiches. They could also get leftover bread from the bakery, coconut water, *acarajé* (shrimp wrapped in fried beans), and *tapioca* (a cheese and/or shredded coconut mixture in a tortilla-type wrap) from vendors they knew.

GUIAS

Guias (tourist guides) range in age from 6 to 26. Girls also work as *guias*, but males dominate as guides. Work as a tourist guide is a status job, primarily because it does not involve physical labor, there is contact with foreigners, and the income is significantly better than vending or other waged work. The fee for tours of the historic district depends on the duration and extent of the tour and is not always negotiated ahead of time. The guides depend on satisfied tourists who will provide extra money, food, or presents in addition to the fee charged for the tour.

Many of the older guides received a training course at an NGO called Guia Mirim, but the organization was closed down after a number of corruption scandals. Trainees discovered that staff was embezzling funds, and they trashed the school. In 1994–95, younger guides received no formal training.

They learn by listening to other guides, or they make up information as they go along. Many perceive that the *gringos* (referring to any foreigner) who hire them don't know if they are providing misinformation, or are unconcerned with historical accuracy, which allows them to make up dates and "facts" that go unchallenged.

Tours take about an hour or so, longer if the tourist stops to eat and drink. Sometimes guides are invited to go on short, local excursions in a taxi, or to spend a longer time with them at some of the local beach resorts, acting as interpreters and companions, including sexual companions. All tourists are presumed wealthy because they can travel, including the backpackers who travel "rough." There is no mechanism for reporting or complaining if a tourist refuses to pay, although a tourist can file a complaint with the tourist police if there is a problem with a guide. Tourists who do not pay (perhaps for an unsatisfactory tour) are "taken care of" later by being assaulted.

Reinaldo, 12, started working at age 6 "*tomando conta dos carros*" (taking care of or watching cars) outside restaurants and bars in the Cidade Alta and on the main road along the coast. His earnings helped support his infirm mother and six siblings. His father was in prison for murder. In addition to his earnings as a guide, he received a commission from a local *pousada*[10] owner for bringing tourists to his place to stay. The owner, Arnaldo, a German and ex-seminarian, lived with his wife, Maria. These two would also provide food, credit, medical, and other assistance to the *guias* in exchange for their "loyalty." Arnaldo would parcel out "points" for the *guias* (like frequent flyer miles), and at the end of the year, the *guia* with the most points received a premium. At Christmas, he always gave a party for the guides. Normally there was no charge, but in 1995, he asked the guides for a donation. The fact that he was able to buy an apartment, maintain his house and car, and afford trips to Germany did not elicit financial support for the holiday party.[11]

The season prior to Carnival and the school holiday season in Brazil and Europe (from June to August) are the peak seasons for earnings. The guides congregate at the Praça do Carmo, the main square where the tourist buses enter the historic district. When tourists disembark, the guides run and knock each other over as they try to convince tourists to use their services. This aggressive marketing at times frightens rather than charms tourists. Four or five may go running after a tourist, making them feel they will be assaulted rather than assisted. Work hours and location are fairly stable (10:00 a.m. to 6:00 p.m., Monday through Saturday), unless they are hired by tourists for extended periods. Egenaldo, age 12, had been working as a guide for two years when I met him, and lived with his family. He became adept at speaking functional Spanish, French, and German.

> I started working by watching cars at night when I was 6 years old. At times, we would not have food every day (for eight people). The next day I would be tired and would not have the energy to go to school. At the time, I didn't know anything about being a *guia*. At about age 10 I started working as a guide, and was going to school in the afternoon. Then I quit school, because if I study I will lose time, time I could spend learning other things.
>
> I live with my family, and I help them out. All of us work, but I am really the *chefe da família* (head of the family). Sometimes I can earn from R$100 to R$200 a week. Sometimes I do not earn anything. I arrive at 7:30 a.m. and stay until 6:00 p.m. I give some of my money to the house, and some [stays] for me. It depends on what we need. I use it to buy clothes, shoes, food, and so on. It is important for me to help my mother. She uses it to buy food, cigarettes, whatever is lacking at home. My brother, age 10, is also a tourist guide and helps too. Especially since my father died. Once in a while I do odd jobs like collect coconuts to sell or maybe paint something for someone or clean their house. When I was 10, my mother gave me to a wealthy lady. I would do odd jobs around her house in exchange for food and she was also going to send me to school. I cried all the time. It didn't work out.
>
> I have to give to my family; I do not have a choice. I see that my family needs it. I could lie about how much I made, and I have. With my money alone this year, we bought a refrigerator and record player, bookshelf, everything new, from a store.
>
> The best thing that ever happened to me was when a French tourist came here and helped me out, gave

me money, talked to me a lot. It was important to me.
Another time I got to know this guy from New York.
He said to call him any time I needed help. It is my
dream to go there and learn English.[12]

I would like to do some work where I could get my
work card signed,[13] have steady work. I would like to
get out of doing this type of work, learn English, work
in a hotel, or as a guide in a travel agency, be a bus driv-
er. I wish I had a bicycle. I wish I could buy something
that would help me earn more money, like a cart to
sell Bar-b-q or something, not something that would
disappear after awhile. Something that would help me
make a profit, but there is nothing certain here.

Another guide, Fofão, was forced to leave his home because of "problems with my stepfather. He didn't like me." He was sent to live with his
aunt. "I was basically one of my aunt's employees, and I think that is exactly why I was given to my aunt." From as far back as he can remember,
he was expected to work and help his family.

When I was six years old, I was selling ice-pops. It was
my aunt who set me up. She bought the styrofoam box
for the ice pops. It was clear to me from the beginning
that I would have to work; there was never any question about it. I was forced, really, and have to say that
I never really liked it. I do not like to sell things on
the street. I always wanted to study, to stay in school.
However, after I moved to my aunt's, they took me out
of school because, basically, if we wanted to eat we had
to work. When I was not selling ice-pops, I was selling *cocada* (a coconut pastry). When I started working
as a *guia*, it was great because, in a way, it was a form
of studying. You had to be interested in the history of
Olinda and Pernambuco. I thought, heh, this could
turn into a real profession. So it did not really matter
that I was not in school, per se. I mean, I taught myself.
It was easy. I got a map and studied.

My uncle works as a *biscateiro*, getting work when he can, but basically, I make more money than anyone else in my family does. I usually give about one-half a minimum salary, even if I make more. For example, this month I only made about half a salary, and I had to give the whole thing. If I make a lot more, I keep it for myself. We spend the money on food, primarily. I use my money for transportation, clothes, shoes, beer, which is my vice.

A normal day is getting up about 7:00 a.m., eating bread and coffee, and then going out to get tourists. I usually arrive about 8:00 a.m. If I don't get any tourists, I just wait. I get home around 5:00 p.m.

It is my aunt who pretty much decides how the money will be spent. She has most of the power, and if I do not give my share, I will be sure to hear her complaining. She has said more than once that what I contribute is nothing, because if I were to rent a house, pay the light, and water and food bills, I could never afford it. And she is right. I really come and go as I please, eat, watch TV, drink cold water.

I really like what I do now, I like talking about the history and folklore of Olinda and Pernambuco. I have always wanted to have a dance academy, and I think about 10 years from now I can do it. What I really want to do is travel outside of Brazil, earn a lot of money, and then come back and do all the things I want. My work is really great because I get to meet all kinds of people, learn a lot of things.

What are the worst and best things that have happened to me? The worst was when my parents separated, then when my father died. My aunt does not love me, I know this. I have no contact at all with my mother. I know where she lives, but she has other children with this other guy, and he doesn't like us very much. I knew that when my aunt took me in it was with another objective, to be her employee.

Fofão did not leave Brazil, but did go to São Paulo for seven years. He returned to Olinda and now heads an NGO with his wife that focuses on teaching and using local culture (dance, theater, music, art) as a community development tool.

Figure 5.8: Vendors. Photo by Janildo.

VENDORS

Some vendors work from fixed locations, such as the bus stop at the Praço do Carmo, the market in Peixinhos, or gas stations. Others peddle their goods on the beach or at one of the numerous bars along the coast. Danada, age 11, sold mixed drinks with her two sisters and mother at the Alta da Sé on Sundays. Edger, age 10, has already worked for two years running a stand at the bus stop that sells candy, gum, cigarettes, coffee, combs, and anything else you might need. He said he tries "to meet the demands of his customers and learn what they need." Unlike the peddlers, Edger's spot puts him in regular contact with customers and allows him to both store and display his merchandise. He works from Monday to Saturday, 6:00 a.m. to 7:00 p.m. taking two hours off for lunch at his uncle's house down the street. When I commented that his work was probably fun because he gets to meet so many people, he responded, "Fun? I hate it. The only day I like is Sunday, which is the only day I don't work. I get to play. I want to go to school." Edger's father has a full-time job as a fare collector on a bus, earning one minimum wage. He told me that he did not intend to keep his son out of school for so long, and "hopefully by next term he can begin again, but right now we need the money."

Figure 5.9: Vendors selling at bus stop. Photo by Janildo.

Jonas, aged 12, sold peanuts on the beach. It was a two-fare, 1-hour ride from São Laurenço to the strip of bars along the beach. He worked from 6:00 p.m. to 2:00 a.m., primarily on weekends. According to Jonas, all his income went to his mother. Although he had an established route, there was no defense against competition from the 10 or so other kids and adults selling peanuts. Vera, aged 6, sold *vatapá* (a shrimp and coconut milk dish) with her mother from a large pot set up close to the bars. She also cleaned houses with her mother. Today she sells *tapioca* (grated cassava that is placed in a circular pan above a makeshift charcoal stove and filled with items such as grated coconut, bananas, sweetened condensed milk, and cheese) with her mother at the Ribeira market in the Cidade Alta.

Figure 5.10: Relaxing in between sales. Photo by Janildo.

LOLÓ

The production, distribution, and consumption of drugs are an additional means for generating or supplementing income. Clebson, aged

12, would make *loló*, a homemade intoxicant made from ether and chloroform. He would buy the solvents at a local pharmacy for R$50 and carefully guard what he called his "secret recipe." *Loló* is cheap, used ubiquitously during Carnival among all classes, and among the lower-class youth the rest of the time. It is made by mixing anesthetic solvents with other ingredients, which may include a sugar/syrup mixture that is necessary to cut the bitter taste of the chloroform. The mixture is then poured into two-inch-high bottles and sold for R$1 each. It is consumed by applying a small amount on a piece of material, usually one's shirt, and then holding it over the nose and breathing deeply until one experiences a sensation similar to anesthetization. The sensation lasts about 15 minutes. I would see numerous young girls faint after sniffing *loló*.

On Sundays, poor youth from the surrounding area flock to the Cidade Alta to dance, flirt, and drink. There is also a large market for *loló* on Sundays, as it is a cheap, effective, and readily available intoxicant. The night would often start with youth sniffing *loló* and slam dancing to Brazilian rap music, until a fight would break out. This would send everyone scattering, for fear of being shot, which would result in airborne tables and chairs. Beer bottles would be broken and used as makeshift weapons. Rocks and bricks would also start flying. The police would then descend, throw all the young men against the wall, lift their shirts to see if they were armed, hit a few of them, check their documents, and haul a few away. After the police had left, the music, dancing, and *loló*-sniffing would continue.

"SEX TOURISM"

The Regional Metropolitan area of Recife (RMR), like parts of Thailand, Sri Lanka, the Philippines, South Korea, and Kenya, is known for its recreational sex industry. Recreational sex clubs are often masked by names such as "beauty salon," "hairdresser," "house for students," or "health club" and are located mainly near the tourist district in Boa Viagem. During the summer months prior to Carnival, about 3,000 women leave their homes and take up temporary residence in a rundown hotel in Boa Viagem in the hopes of securing a "summer love" with a wealthy tourist. The Secretary of

Industry, Commerce, and Tourism for Pernambuco stated, "It is not important if the tourist spends his dollars with prostitutes or in the deluxe hotels or in the shopping center. The thing is that they leave their dollars here." Since 2004, a number of airlines now provide direct flights from European capitals to Recife.

Prostitution is legal in Brazil after the age of 18, although it is estimated that eighty per cent of the girls are under the age of 20.[14] A number of the more than 200 massage parlors, rooms, pension houses, bars, and striptease nightclubs use minors to attract clients because clients feel they are "clean," free of disease. One proprietor stated, "When I changed four of my eight girls for four girls under 17, my profits increased. It's easy to find them. The police can come in. It's a private club. They like it. They don't ask their ages."[15] The age of consent in Brazil is 14 (sex with a girl under this age is considered rape) although someone can be charged with "corruption of minors" (adolescents between 14 and 18) if the parent or minor files a complaint. Although a number of countries criminalize sex with minors, monitoring and enforcement are extremely difficult.

According to the World Travel and Tourism Council (2007), tourism represents over 11 per cent of the world's gross domestic product (GDP) and over 8 per cent of world employment. In 2004, international tourism revenues totaled about $623 billion. In Brazil, tourism accounted for approximately 5.5 per cent of Brazil's GDP (Blake 2005: 24).It is one of the fastest growing and least regulated industries, noted primarily for its violation of labor laws.

Brazil has experienced major growth in tourism since the 1990s (Mamede, 1996). Just in the first quarter of 2006, tourists spent an estimated US $2 billion. In 2003, President Lula created a Ministry of Tourism that is charged with monitoring and evaluating the tourism sector, as well as providing support for tourism as an income-generating activity.

In 1994, the Northeast Tourism Program PRODETUR/NE-I was granted a US$400 million loan from the Interamerican Development Bank (IDB) for Tourism Development. Funding targeted mostly infrastructure development in coastal communities (Hinchberger, 2005). Although economists tend to assert the positive impact of tourism-employment, diffusion of crafts, music, and food-tourism in Northeast Brazil seems directed at mostly the development of the "sun, sand, sea, sex, and subservience" forms of tourism (Crick, 1996). Benefits are channeled mostly to individual entrepreneurs and a small elite, rather than contributing to overall community development (Slob & Wilde, 2006; Prado, 2003). Jobs are created, but mostly for young and attractive waiters, waitresses, cooks, and tourist guides. There are a number of cases where a lack of community control and input over tourism development has resulted in environmental degradation, loss of land, and commodification of culture. Since 1992, the recognition of Pelourinho, in Salvador, Bahia, as a UNESCO World Heritage Site, has created a lucrative tourism industry. The historic district has been transformed from a poor barrio to a tourist magnet for "authentic Afro-Brazilian culture" which ironically has expulsed its authentic poor, black residents. Olinda, another World Heritage Site, also calls into question the value of tourism if the poor are spatially excluded from historic districts, or when income, racial, ethnic, and gendered inequities are increased.

In general, the young women who have sexual relationships with foreign tourists do not have a fixed price for "services," do not identify as sex workers, and do not describe what they do as an "occupation." Sexual relationships with foreigners is just one strategy among many for dealing with poverty, as well as the desire for travel and other material goods. It is often one of the only available economic niches open to poor females. Sometimes they establish long-term relationships with partners, who send money and gifts and return year after year. As one young woman said, "I don't have anything to lose, and besides, I earn more than a teacher does here."

I was frequently approached by girls, barely over 12, who saw me as a link to setting them up with foreign male tourists. They would give me photographs of themselves scantily clad, and ask me to show it to gringos and arrange "get togethers." When I provided disposable cameras to some of the young girls I knew and asked them to take photographs of daily life in the favela, they took photographs of each other naked instead. I had the film developed locally, and feared that I would be reported to the police for "sex trafficking" when I saw the types of photographs they had taken. The girls were puzzled and disappointed when I refused to show the photographs to foreign males looking for a Brazilian "girlfriend." They preferred foreigners to Brazilian men because they "treat us better." Foreign males in Olinda were usually on vacation, and had disposable income for recreation and gifts, unlike local males. A number of 14-year-old girls I knew from V8 worked at the Inferninho on Sundays, but were never able to garner much money, given that their "clients" were paying less than a dollar for services. Most of the clients and girls were from the same favela. Tara, aged 15, who lived with both her parents, said she would *only* have sex with gringos and always asked them for at least R$50. "If I ask for only R$30, I have to receive something else, like a blouse. I never, ever, have sex without getting something in return."

Initially, I concluded that relationships between foreign men and young Brazilian women reflected geopolitical, racial, economic, gendered, and age inequities. I assumed the women lacked agency and were just pawns in a global market that exploits the bodies of the poor as laborers and commodities. The partners of some of the women are often old enough to be their grandfathers. Brazilian bodies, both male and female, are marketed internationally as alluring and available, and males were specific about finding a dark-skinned "Cinderella of the Sand" (Sonhos de Verão, 1995, p. 38). I would see the young women washing the clothes, making meals and cleaning the houses of their foreign boyfriends. Yet the same characteristics that feminists have criticized as contributing to women's exploitation (servile, dependent), "pay" in the tourist industry. The young women felt they are sought after because they are sexier, more affectionate, and attentive than career-driven, foreign, white women. They insisted they were treated better by foreign males, as local men were "*machistas*" and expected them to be servile and feminine, without any financial benefit. In many ways, these girls/women were using the global process of tourism to garner resources in the short term, with the hope that additional opportunities, such as travel, education, and work, would be forthcoming. They commented on the "lucky" ones who married foreigners who took them back to Germany, France, Italy, England, Spain, and Holland.

There are numerous horror stories, some documented, some anecdotal and unsubstantiated, of "trafficked" women trapped in abusive relationships and forced to work in the sex industry. However, the young women I knew who had left Brazil with their "summer loves" were for the most part happy with their decisions, even though they were working as maids, waitresses, topless dancers, or not at all, and were faced with loneliness and isolation. They still felt it was better than their prospects in Brazil. Lacking formal education and a financial safety net, they could at least travel back and forth, provide money for their families, and felt they had some status in relation to their peers. More systematic research on sexual relationships between middle- and upper-class males and females and foreign tourists is necessary. Sex between poor males and females and tourists, which is often interracial as well, is almost immediately labeled as "sex tourism" and seen as absent of love, affection or desire, whereas relationships between those with means is seen as "legitimate," less exploitative, and based on "real" love and affection and not "strategic" or utilitarian motives. Exploration of the nature, extent, and "strategic use" of relationships between those with means would perhaps show some overlap of characteristics seen as exclusive to the "sex tourism" industry.

SCHOOL AND WORK

Attending school full time, even for a short period, is a luxury most families cannot afford, as it means a loss of earnings. It interferes with domestic tasks, such as child care, cleaning, cooking, doing errands, fetching water, sweeping, and washing clothes, or is at odds with peak work hours. In order to optimize earnings, children may attend school on alternate days, or one is sent one day and another on a different day. Many attend school diligently the first few weeks, only to drop out after the first month and say with resignation, "I'll never make it," or "Maybe next year." Education is highly valued, but material need outweighs the advantage of keeping children in school, especially when local conditions offer immediate and tangible remunerative opportunities for children. In a survey carried out by the Centro Luiz Freire in 1996, 45 per cent of the parents they interviewed in Pernambuco said that the need to work was the chief reason for their children not attending school. Work experience is also seen as qualifying kids for the jobs they will most likely end up getting anyway, even though physical/manual labor is associated with low wages and low social status, despite the skill level.

Public schooling is free and compulsory between the ages of 7 and 14. There is significant evidence showing a positive correlation between education, income, and quality of life. Yet increasingly, higher qualifications are required for jobs with even mediocre wages.

In Pernambuco, there has been significant growth in the service sector (especially tourism), specialized medical services, insurance, and the financial industry, all requiring additional time spent in school. Although illiteracy in the Northeast decreased from 55 per cent in 1970 to 36 per cent in 1989, other areas of the country showed more significant reductions at the same time that formal education became an essential requirement for accessing a job. In Olinda, according to the 2000 census, the level of illiteracy among the 11–14 age group fell from 13.6 per cent in 1991, to 6.46 per cent in 2000. For those above age 15, the level of illiteracy fell from 14.8 per cent in 1991, to 9.93 per cent in 2000. However, those who have managed to complete some schooling do not necessarily have an advantage. Those with little or no formal study and those who have completed four years of schooling "substitute" each other, meaning they compete equally against each other for the same jobs, and there is little differential in earnings (Griffen & Edwards, 1993, p. 252).

Those who can afford it send their kids to one of the many private schools in the area, at the cost of about US$2,500 per year (about 37 minimum wages).[16] The rest attend public schools that are notorious for having poorly remunerated, unmotivated, and untrained teachers. Classes are overcrowded, and chronic strikes and lack of resources contribute to a precarious learning environment. On average, kids take 12 years, instead of 8, to complete primary school (Szanton-Blanc, 1994). Many begin their schooling late, abandon courses in the middle of the year and later resume their studies in the same grade, or simply fail to pass. The Northeast has the highest concentration of older students in school: 90 per cent of all children over 10 are behind in their studies and 87 per cent of all high-school students are over 18 (Rizzini, Rizzini, Muñoz-Vargas, & Galeano, 1994). There are 1.4 million children who do not attend school at all.

The children I met attended school sporadically and then stopped completely. Edna, a beggar, would cringe when she saw other 10-year-olds on the streets and say, "I feel ashamed. I have to put my head down. I can't look at them. I see the kids of the tourists, rich Brazilians, staring at me. They look so nice, all dressed in nice clothes." She dropped out of school after she failed the last exam. "You know, the teacher was the one who bought the notebook for me. It was ripped up by my little brother. How can I go back to school without a notebook? And nothing to write with. Besides, I'm too hungry to go to school. I am always having stomach pains. And I've missed too many days anyway, so what's the point in going to school hungry? When I do not eat, my stomach hurts, I cannot seem to stand the hunger as much as the babies even. Even after I eat it hurts for a long time."

Figure 5.11: Edna (*right*), 1994: "I'm too hungry to go to school." Photo by author.

Rosemarie, another beggar, aged 12, was excited by school. She was a bright and promising pupil, yet household demands eclipsed school attendance. "All the other kids at school just want to fool around; they draw on the walls, but not me. I want to study, and the teacher knows that. But I stopped going. I didn't have the materials to study. I didn't like it anymore. I missed so many days, and they took me off the list." Although public schooling is "free," they require uniforms and other materials, which children must buy, increasing rather than decreasing their labor.

Figure 5.12: Edna with her son, 2002. Photo by Edna's partner, João.

CONCLUSION

Responses to poverty are context-specific and heterogeneous. Not all poor families rely on children's earnings, and many poor families felt that putting one's kids to work was "immoral."

> Sending your kids out to work is wrong. They learn from a young age that this is a way of getting money. Why don't their parents work? Why don't they knock on doors and offer to do anything at all, cut grass, clean the yard, wash clothes? It is common here to borrow kids for begging. Put your 14-year-old together with your neighbor's 2-year-old, and both families split the earnings. And they beg because otherwise they will be beaten. And most likely the food is for the father, although the kids do it for their mothers, for sure. They do not want to see her go hungry. *The head of the house is a child.* They go out in the morning, bring home the lunch, go out again, bring home the dinner. They are the breadwinners. They are very good at getting money, and the parents know it and make kids to go out and work for them.

One day I asked Gloria why her kids work. She responded by weaving a narrative about intergenerational hardship and economic strategizing in a context of scarcity.

> I have always suffered. Suffered when I was a little kid, until today. I don't know my real mother. My stepmother raised me. I arrived at her house when I was three months old. My real mother knew my step-father because they worked together at the same market. When my mother was pregnant with me, she told him that when I am born, she was going to give me away because she didn't have the means to raise me. I know that I have a lot of brothers and sisters, but I have never met them. So a man my mother knew

decided to take me, because he only had one child. After I was born, my mother put me in a sack, and gave me to him. He put me together with his bananas and took me to his house. The first person to bathe me was my stepmother. She said she was repulsed when she saw me because I was so filthy. I guess my mother had never bathed me. My stepmother treated me badly and I am not going to lie and say I lived well. She would beat me. Everyone in the neighborhood knew this. She eventually kicked me out of the house when I was about 15.

This was the same time I met my husband. I was working as a maid at that time in Casa Caiada (a neighborhood in Olinda). My stepparents made me work since I was 12 years old. My stepmother never gave me anything. I was always using borrowed clothes, used clothes. People used to feel sorry for me.

I am still with my husband today, after 13 years. I have to save food for him, or the kids will eat everything. I suffer with him. He's a brute, but I stay with him because of these kids. If I had a mother who helped me, I would not be here. My real mother would have helped me. My husband lies. And with the littlest things, he gets mad and beats me. [Her daughter, age 10, is listening and confirming what she is saying and also putting in her own two cents.] He drinks and fights with me. [Her daughter says, "He tried to stab her."] Why do I put up with this? I wouldn't if I had some help. He is a great person, just very agitated, gets upset easily. He's 37 and I'm 28. I do everything. He demands, and I give. Give me this, give me that. I don't think many people here live this way, it is uncommon. I already left him twice, but returned because I have all these kids to raise. If I leave him, these girls will go wild. I want to leave him. I don't have a good life. Oh sure, my husband always kept an eye on us, kept us near wherever he was working. He

gets odd jobs, whenever he can. Right now, he is lay-
ing bricks for a house around the corner. For a while,
we lived here without a wall, it was completely open.
I have lived with this man for 13 years, and we don't
have anything. Even though he is working, he is not
the type of man to say, "Look. I made this much. Take
this and use it for clothes." I do not have clothes to
go out in, or shoes. [She tells her daughter to shut up
because she is interrupting.]

So, this is my life. Only suffering. And I don't
think it is going to change very much. I do not think
there exists a person with more patience than me.
Even today, I went at 4:00 a.m. to the health post, to
the dentist, to get on line to get a *ficha*.[7] When I finally got to the dentist, there was no water, no equipment, no dentist, always something. Most women get
all bent out of shape, but I never complain. I try to
stay calm. I adapt to the good and the bad. No one is
really to blame.

I asked her how her kids started working.

My neighbor told me about places where kids can work.
Her kids had already been working for a while. We were
homeless for a while, and lived in front of the city hall.
The baby was sick. We would sleep on the street. People
would give us food and other things, and then one day
someone took us to a shelter. We stayed there for three
months, but after that, they put us out. So we collected
garbage for a while to get by, cans and stuff. Later, we
arrived here [in the favela].

One day when we weren't doing anything my
neighbor said, "Let's go up there and ask tourists for
money. They give to the kids." So we cleaned our-
selves up and gave the kids a bath and off we went.
The first time we did it, we got about five *reais*. I went
by the supermarket on the way home and bought

coffee and some stuff for the kids and I thought, heh, this is pretty good. [At this point, her 10-year-old daughter starts talking, and Gloria tells her to shut up, that she is rude.] After about the third time, the kids said, "This time we are going alone." And I said, "No way. It's too dangerous. You could be kidnapped or something." "No, it's not," they said. "Everyone knows us." And I realized that it was the littlest one who was getting the most money. So I let them go alone, until today. My girls like to go, at times do not tell, even tell their father.

What do I spend the money on? Food, cookies, shampoo, cream rinse, soap, bananas, and milk. Sometimes I buy alcohol to cook with. My husband is always walking around looking for work. Sometimes he gets it, sometimes no. But every day he goes out looking. My kids work because they don't want to see me go hungry. But they also go because there's nothing to do here.

Sometimes they earn somethin', sometimes no. I am not going to kill them for that. No way. God decides what will happen with all of us. Sometimes they earn enough for us to get by. Sometimes I have to go out looking for them if they stay out too long. I get worried, especially about the one who is almost a *moça*. The men will be after her. I don't know anything, really, about this area. The kids know more than I do, they know the streets, the different areas. I don't even go out.

I asked her if she ever thought about letting the kids take the two-year-old with them, given the apparent success in getting money.

This one? Oh, no way. This one is a *child of God*. He was born sickly. Didn't have the force to live. Even the doctor said, "He is already in God's hands.' So I prayed and prayed and all of a sudden he just started smiling and

> moving and miraculously got better, which is why he
> does not have any godparents because Jesus and Mary
> are his godparents.

During this conversation, the "child of god" woke up crying. She handed him a plastic bowl filled with *mingau* (porridge), and he sat on the bed and ate and drank water from a cup full of holes. I asked him, "And what are you eating that you are getting so big?" "Water," he shot back. A few minutes late, his mother notices the time (4:00 p.m.), and tells the other children, "Its time to go to work. Go on," she urges them. "I don't want to go," the four-year-old whines, then kisses her mother before taking the hand of the second youngest, and they head out the door.

On numerous occasions Gloria tells me, "I am not going to keep them doing this forever; just until we can pull something together. It is so difficult here because if you don't know someone, you can't get a job. If you just knock on someone's door, they think you are there to rob them. There is no work here. I want to work, really. I want to take my girls off the street. It's dangerous. But right now we have no other option."

A few years later, her eldest son is shot in a dispute over payment for drugs. He had already been shot at twice before, but survived and left the favela for a neighboring city. He is later shot while drinking a beer in a bar on the outskirts of the city.

Gloria decided it was time to leave the favela and try their luck elsewhere. She contacted a cousin in Rio, and with her youngest son, aged two, went to stay with her. The rest of the children, aged 10–20, stayed behind with her husband. A few weeks later, he sold their house for 800 *reais* (about US$400), bought a bus ticket to Rio, and left the rest of the children behind, promising to send for them as soon as he and Gloria were settled. When I last saw them, the 15-year-old was pregnant and periodically living on the street. The eldest girl had taken off to the interior with a new boyfriend, while the second oldest, now 19, with two children of her own, supported the rest of the family on her salary as a maid, making about 600 *reais* (US$300) a month. They were sharing a two-room house with her sister and her sister's boyfriend. It had been three months since she had heard from her parents. "I know they'll send

95

for us soon. As soon as they can. I have to get out of this favela. They are they only family I've got."

Figure 5.13: Gloria: "I'm not going to keep them doing this forever.
Just until we can pull something together."

NOTES

1. Evelyn Blackwood (2005) challenges the pervasive "heteronormativity" in social science research, and calls for a gendered analysis of "missing man" labels (female-headed households, matrifocal) in order to provide a more nuanced understanding of relatedness and household formation and functioning.

2. Leptospirosis is a bacterial disease that causes headaches, fevers, chills, and rashes. It is caused by exposure to water that has been contaminated with the urine of animals (in urban Brazil it is usually rats) carrying the bacteria. During the rainy season, the number of persons infected with leptospirosis increases dramatically, as they wade through stagnant, muddy water.

3. In 1992, UNICEF began providing education, nutrition, and recreation programs for children in the *lixão*. It was a UNICEF program officer who first took me to the *lixão* in 1995. In 2003, Susan Sarandon came to the Olinda *lixão* as UNICEF's goodwill ambassador and made a film, *What's Going On?*, about child labor in Brazil.

4. She eventually met another man and moved with him to the interior, where he works at a car repair shop.

5. A Likert scale is a research method/tool often used in social science questionnaires that assesses respondent reaction to statements with closed-ended "levels" of agreement, such as "strongly agree, agree," and so on.

6. Literally, "dental floss" bathing suits made famous by Brazilian women.

7. This is exactly what happened. In 1999, Dalva got pregnant and moved out of her mother's house.

8. See Curtis, R.F. (1986). Household and family in theory on inequality. *American Sociological Review, 51*, 168; Harris, M., & Ross, E.B. (1987). *Death, sex and fertility: Population regulation in preindustrial and developing societies.* New York: Columbia University Press; Van Esterik, P. (1985). Intrafamily food distribution: Its relevance for maternal and child nutrition. Cornell Nutritional Surveillance Program. In *Determinants of young child feeding and their implications for nutritional surveillance* (pp. 74–149). Ithaca, NY: Cornell University Program in International Nutrition, Cornell International Nutrition Monograph series, no. 14; Gross, D., & Underwood, B.A. (1971). Technological

change and caloric costs. *American Anthropologist*, 73, 725–40; Gonzalez de la Rocha, M. (1995). The urban family and poverty in Latin America. *Latin American Perspectives*, 85(2), 22.

9. In his study of street youth in Brazil, Hecht (1998) found that they could eat more and better than they would at home.

10. *Pousadas* are guesthouses or small hotels. In Olinda, they range from youth hostels that charge about US$5 for a bed in a dormitory with a shared bathroom, to luxurious suites in renovated houses in the Cidade Alta with pools and wine cellars.

11. The *pousada* has since closed. The owner bought a house at the beach, then separated from his wife and moved to Mexico.

12. I tried to help him contact this "friend" from New York. When we called him, the tourist was suspicious and told me he wanted nothing to do with the guide.

13. *Carteira assinada* is a work card signed by an employer, which indicates one is a formal worker eligible for benefits.

14. A study conducted by Ana Rosa Lehmann-Carpzov (1984), *Turismo e Identidade—formação de identidades Sociais entre Mulheres Brasileiras and Homens Alemães no Contexto do Turismo Sexual na Cidade do Recife*, examined the sex tourism industry involving German nationals and Brazilian women in Recife. Unpublished master's thesis, Department of Anthropology, Universidade Federal do Pernambuco.

15. São infernos lotados de menores. (1992, 26 January). *Jornal do Comercio*, caderno C, 1.

16. Crise não atinge as escolas particulares. (1996, May 23). *Jornal do Comercio*, p. 6.

17. To access services at the public health clinic one must get on a line and get a number (*ficha*). A finite number of *fichas* are given out daily. People sleep outside the clinic the night before in order to obtain an advantageous place in line. Strikes and a lack of resources and personnel complicate service provision.

CHAPTER SIX
STREET CHILDREN IN NORTHEAST BRAZIL

In this chapter I explore a popular label (street child) used to describe and differentiate children. Children who work *in* the street are called *meninos/as na rua* and are "housed" in some way, regardless of the precarious conditions in which they live. "Street children" (*meninos/as da rua*) are those who eke out a living on the street, are assumed to be "unattached" to their natal family, and are in general defined by what they lack. Both labels homogenize children's experiences, their backgrounds, the nature and extent of contact with their families, and access to resources.

Regional differences, economic conditions, means of survival, social relations, levels of violence, social assistance, and changes in laws and policies all affect the configuration of the "street child" and the number of children on the street during a particular period. A more nuanced understanding of the lives of young street dwellers requires extensive contact with children in a particular area in order to assess their views on homelessness and/or abandonment. For example, Hecht (1998) found that young street dwellers in urban Northeast Brazil do not adopt the label "street kid" until they sever all ties—emotional, physical, and economic—with their *mothers*. Cutting ties with one's mother means they have adopted "bad" (street) behaviors and have failed to live a righteous life. Even then, identity as a street child shifts based on the context, using the "street kid" label primarily with adults and social welfare agents, and "wild one" with one another. The author suggests that sensationalism trumps evidence for massive numbers of abandoned children on the streets in Latin America. Instead, social welfare agencies play a "numbers game," citing phantom sources and research studies that exaggerate the severity of the problem (Hecht, 1998, pp. 101–02). Other studies show that the pathway out of the home, whether imposed or chosen, is a process, and due to a cluster of cumulative handicaps: poverty, and sexual and physical violence (Body-Bendrot, 2000). In Brazil, Rizzini, Muñoz-Vargas, and Galeano (1992) found that homeless children come not from the poorest families, but those with the highest levels of physical abuse.

Whenever I asked kids why they were living on the street, they inevitably said things were "bad at home, so I left." In one study with 1000 street girls, about half said they left home between the ages of 12–16. Eighteen per cent said they left because of problems with their mother, 24 per cent to get their own money. Other reasons included pregnancy, death of a parent, and abandonment. Half reported they engaged in sexual relationships in exchange for money or food and 95 per cent received "help from someone." The rest washed windshields at stoplights and stole (Vasconcelos, 1992). Most street dwellers are male, aged 7–17 (Rizzini & Rizzini, 1991). In studies that note "color," almost all are brown or Black. In Recife, they are popularly referred to as *cheira cola* (glue sniffers).

Views concerning "what to do" with abandoned children are varied and shift with changes in administration, social welfare policy, and human rights standards. The practice of child "circulation" or abandonment has a long history in Europe (since the twelfth century) and in colonial Latin America.[1] Since the fifteenth century, states have taken steps to care for abandoned children, although there was an implicit expectation that the majority of infants would die in institutional care.[2] During the eighteenth century, almost a quarter of all children born in urban areas in Brazil were abandoned, and 80 per cent died before the age of seven. In 1726, the *Roda dos Expostos* (foundling wheel) provided residents of Salvador, Bahia (having already been used in Portugal) an anonymous vehicle for "depositing" unwanted children. The wheel resembled a large cylinder embedded in the wall of a foundling home, with one side exposed to the street. The infant was placed in the cylinder and the cylinder was turned, with the opening then facing the internal part of the home. When it turned, it rang a bell, signaling a new arrival (Venâncio, 1999). Wet-nurses employed by the foundling homes were usually poor, malnourished, and lived far from the home. Boys were recruited from foundling homes to work as apprentices, rural laborers, or urban factory workers, while girls were recruited to work as domestics. Although the numbers were small, parents could reclaim their children (Guimarães Sá, 2000). Little is known about the fate of those who survived to adulthood (Kertzer, 2000, p. 42).

This *Roda dos Expostos*, although not a spinning wheel in a wall, still functions in a number of countries ("baby hatches" of Germany or "safe havens" in the United States). Children are also "given" to others to repay favors or to reduce the number of dependents, or "triaged" to households where it is more likely they can attend school or earn money in exchange for labor.[3] Those who secure jobs as maids, for example, have at least the potential for securing a patron in exchange for their labor. Although viewed benignly as an adopted *agregados* (unrelated household member), the kids I knew in this situation felt they were servants, not members of the family.[4] Sometimes parents hope that their kids will wind up in a state or religious institution, or some other form of residential care. Neto's mother "let her son go" to the street, saying, "He is just too wild, untamable. He has always been that way. I could never control him." Although he did spend some time in a church-associated residential institution for delinquent boys learning how to tend goats, he eventually got into an argument with another resident and ran away. Today he sleeps in the cemetery.

Much of the random violence that occurs on urban streets is blamed on street kids. Subsequently, they are easy targets for control, containment, and violence, and detained on imprecise grounds such as "loitering" or "vagrancy" (Boyden, 1990, p. 209). In February 2006, the police forced a number of "vagrant" adolescents to jump off a bridge in Joana Bezerra, Recife. Two drowned as a result.[5] In her ethnographic study of the city of São Paulo, Brazil, Teresa Caldeira (1992) notes how the fear of random violence has enveloped the "ordinary" citizen, even though most of the victims of crime are poor, young, and Black (Soares & Borges, 2004, p. 28). Alba Zaluar, a Brazilian anthropologist who studies urban violence, found that 70 per cent of violent deaths in Brazil happen to those between the ages of 15 and 17; 50 per cent are due to death squads, 40 per cent to drug traffickers, and 8.5 per cent from the police. The 15–19 age group registers the highest number of assassinations, with more than 45,000 killed in 15 years.[6] In 2000, there was a 77 per cent increase in the number of adolescents killed compared to the 1990s.[7] In Recife, "Don't kill my children" is painted on walls and printed on T-shirts. Begging and sniffing glue leads to police harassment, as does testifying and talking back. On February 20, 1997, in Belford Roxo, 15 kilometers from Rio de Janeiro, three security guards of a bus company shot and killed three youths after they made a disturbance on the bus and refused to pay their fare.

Figure 6.1: "Don't kill our children." Source: GAJOP (Gabinete de assessorial Jurídica às organizações populares Centro Luiz Freire). (1991). *Grupos de Extermínio: A Banalização da vida e da morte em Pernambuco.*

Anthropologist Mary Douglas's description of "risky" is apt for popular views of street children: menacing and polluting. They are metaphors for what she defines as "dirt" or "matter out of place" (Douglas, 1994, p. 46; Douglas, 1966). They are people out of place, dirt on the urban landscape and symbols of disorder (Scheper-Hughes & Hoffman, 1998, p. 383). Unlike most of the poor segregated in the favelas, they challenge use of public space. "Anti-street people architecture," such as gates, guards, electric fences, iron bars, and showerheads, attempt to keep street dwellers from using public space (Pereira Lima, 1997). The fear of violence in urban areas, coupled with distrust of "official" forms of law enforcement, has created a thriving industry in privatized safety. In São Paulo, a third of its 35 million residents pay guards to watch over their homes (Huggins & Macturk, 2000), while the poor are "policed" by drug traffickers in the favelas (Pinheiro, 1996). Merchants feel that street youth are a nuisance, that their presence interferes with business, and wish that they would just "disappear": "Business is slow, because of them. They are all thieves. They make violence. They rob and kill. That is why you should take every one of them and kill them, one by one." They are outraged that Brazilian law protects minors from being tried as adults: "They just get away with crimes." "These kids need to be taught about law and order," a police officer told me. He felt his job was to "pull the problem out by the root."[8] Others insist that capital punishment is the only effective deterrent to crime, despite the evidence showing otherwise.

Police involvement in criminal activity is well known in Brazil. Kids I knew were threatened if they did not steal for the police, or turn over stolen goods. "It's not even worth stealing a watch because the cop would expect you to give it to him," José told me. Interestingly, in Dimenstein's (1991) study of violence against children, 30 per cent said they would like to be a policeman when they grow up so that "they could steal without getting caught" (p. 60). Efforts to prosecute police are almost impossible, lengthy, and result in light sentences. Fear and mistrust of the police and justice system, of "disappearing" by police, private security guards, or death squads, efficiently cuts off any actions toward accountability. Private security guards and death squads also "cleanse" the streets of poor children. One case that received international attention occurred on July 23, 1993, when police randomly shot at a group of about 50 children between the ages of 10 and 17 sleeping outside the Candelaria Church in Rio de Janeiro. Four died immediately and two others died in the hospital. Six others were injured. One survivor/witness of this massacre moved to Switzerland (with the help of an NGO) in order to protect his life. Another was killed on November 22, 1996, in a favela in Rio. Then in June 2000, police asphyxiated another survivor after he held hostage a busload of passengers for six hours in Rio. Five other survivors have since died.

According to one shop owner, "Nobody wants kids to get killed. The problem is that there is no other solution. If they are arrested, the courts just let them go and they are free to steal again, which puts my shop under threat. Don't I have the right to run my shop in peace? There is a need to solve this problem, even with unconventional methods" (Dimenstein, 1991, p. 64). Those who defend the position of minors are portrayed as attacking the rights of "decent" people. These are "risky" children, not children at risk (Stephens, 1995, p. 13). They are not seen as children any more, as their behavior is "outside" the boundaries of childhood (Jenks, 1998, p. 128). One ex-death squad member explained:

> What happens is you are employed by a group of shop-keepers. You earn more than a police officer. A boy comes along and robs the shop, so you give him a thump. Another comes along and steals something else. If you don't do anything and let them go on stealing, you lose your job. It's no use playing about with some of these kids. You've got to kill them. (Dimenstein, 1991, p. 44)

Adalgesia, an exchange student from Guinea-Bissau I befriended who lived in a luxury apartment in Boa Viagem, despised street kids. "I don't know why you try to talk to them. They will eventually just rip you off. You're just foolish and naive. They only reason they hang around you is because you have money. There are a lot of them where I come from, and frankly, if they steal anything, I think they should be executed."

People in the US have often asked me, "Why do Brazilians murder street kids?" This distancing of "violent others" both essentializes abuse by attributing it to nationality and/or culture while ignoring the ubiquity of child abuse, exploitation, and structural violence in the United States that foment violence. In fact, the US executes more juveniles than any country in the world.[9]

The *Child and Adolescent Rights Act* (1990) states that minors who commit crimes can be sent to state detainment centers called *Fundação Estadual do Bem-Estar do Menor* (FEBEM), for up to three years.[10] Since 1964 these penal/correctional institutions for minors are charged with social rehabilitation, "keeping an eye" on young offenders, and protecting them from violence by vigilante groups. However, the centers are notorious for the widespread use of torture and ill-treatment,[11] dramatized in Hector Babenco's 1980 film *Pixote*. "They kill children there [at FEBEM].... Why do you think they built it so close to the cemetery?" (Scheper-Hughes & Hoffman, 1994). The number of interned is well beyond capacity, breakouts and riots are common, and staff salaries are delayed for months. In Pernambuco, more than 50 per cent of the offenders who leave the centers are later arrested.[12] One 13-year-old female street dweller told me that the police tend to "leave us alone because we have something to give them," meaning they perform oral sex on officers in exchange for not being sent to FEBEM. Their arms are covered with scars, visual reminders of where they had cut themselves in order to be taken to the hospital instead of to the police station.[13]

As with other marginalized populations worldwide, the internalization of the rhetoric of "personal deficiency" eclipses attention to structural inequities. During a meeting convened to discuss program development for street youth, one of the coordinators was exasperated by the "lax attitude" among street youth and said they "should take on more responsibility." I suggested that the problem was perhaps not personal pathology but the priority of securing immediate means of survival. He quickly shot back, "Your pretty words and intellectualizing are very nice, thank you, but we are the ones putting up the money."

Some programs encourage adoption of street kids, but they are charity-oriented (providing food, clothing, and time, like the Big Brother/Sister program in the US), not legal adoptions. Other interventions target reproduction among the poor as a means to prevent unwanted pregnancies. Having children they neither want nor can afford, leads to ineffective and/or incompetent socialization (an aspect of their "culture of poverty"), ultimately creating bad childhoods, criminals, and the abandoned. It also asserts an association between low fertility, stable income, and higher wages.[14]

Eleven-year-old Negão would say that street kids are "difficult" to work with, that it takes years to "get any results." "The only solution to the problem is to get a gun and kill everyone, then myself. Then start all over." Street kids view their early mortality as predictable and natural, like an occupational hazard. They are killed because they are bad, not normal, "off track," as Hecht argues. They live the life of vagabonds rather than the righteous life and must pay for their sins (Hecht, 1998, pp. 109–12).

NOTES

1. See Guimarães Sá, I. dos. (2000). Circulation of children in eighteenth-century Portugal. In C. Panter-Brick & M.T. Smith (Eds.), *Abandoned children* (pp. 27–40). Cambridge: Cambridge University Press; Boswell, J.

(1988). *The kindness of strangers: The abandonment of children in Western Europe from late antiquity to the Renaissance.* Harmondsworth: Penguin; Modell, J. (1978). Patterns of consumption, acculturation, and family income strategies in late nineteenth-century America. In T.K. Hareven & M.A. Vinovskis (Eds.), *Family and population in nineteenth-century America* (pp. 220–25). Princeton: Princeton University Press.

2. See Smith, M.T. (1999). Modeling the economic and human costs of foundling care in the Azores. In C. Panter-Brick & M.T. Smith (Eds.), *Abandoned children* (pp. 57–69). Cambridge: Cambridge University Press; Viazzo, P.P., Bortolotto, M., & Zanotto, A. (1999). Five centuries of foundling history in Florence: Changing patterns of abandonment, care, and mortality. In C. Panter-Brick & M.T. Smith (Eds.), *Abandoned children* (pp. 70–91). Cambridge: Cambridge University Press.

3. See Fonseca, C. (1986). Orphanages, foundlings and foster mothers: the system of child circulation in a Brazilian squatter settlement. *Anthropological Quarterly*, 59, 5–27; Guimarães Sá, I. dos. (2000). Circulation of children in eighteenth-century Portugal. In C. Panter-Brick & M.T. Smith (Eds.), *Abandoned children* (pp. 27–40). Cambridge: Cambridge University Press; Perlberg (1986) found that parents and husbands who committed wives and children to mental hospitals felt they needed to hand control over to a stronger authority and that they lacked the ability to control them. Cited in La Fontaine (1986). An anthropological perspective on children in social worlds. In M. Richards & P. Light (Eds.), *Children of social worlds: Development in a social context.* Cambridge: Polity, referring to Perlberg, R.J. (1986).*Family and mental illness in a London borough.* Unpublished doctoral dissertation, London University.

4. See Cadet, J.R. (1998). *Restavèc: From Haitian slave child to middle-class American.* Austin: University of Texas Press, for an autobiographical account of contemporary Haitian slavery.

5. Comitê vê subnotificação de tortura pela polícia. *Diario de Pernambuco*, 2006, June 27 p. B6.

6. Assassinations triple in Brazil during 15 year period. (1996, 14 November). SEJEP (Serviço Brasileiro de Justiça e Paz), no. 252.

7. See *Human rights violations in Brazil: An NGO report to the United Nations Human Rights Committee*, by CEDECA/BA—The Yves de Roussan Defense Center for Children and Adolescents, *CLADEM*—The Latin

American and Caribbean Committee for the Defense of Women's Rights, and *FIDDH*—The Inter-American Foundation for the Defense of Human Rights. Geneva (2005, 17 October–4 November), p. 32.

8. This was also reflected in journalist Gilberto Dimenstein (1991). *Brazil: War on children*. London: Latin America Bureau.

9. Totenberg, N. (2004, October 13). Supreme Court hears juvenile death penalty case. *Morning edition* [Radio broadcast]. National Public Radio.

10. The name was changed to FUNDAC (*Fundação Estadual da Criança e do Adolescente*) in 1994.

11. *Brazil: Briefing on Brazil's second periodic report on the implementation of the International Covenant on Civil and Political Rights.* (2005, October). Retrieved October 27, 2005 from <http://web.amnesty.org/library/print/ENGAMR190212005>, p. 8. Interned adolescents at the FEBEM in Tatuapé made a CD with the Brazilian rap group Jigaboo in 2004 where they express their feelings about life in FEBEM. Retrieved from <http://www.buxixo.com.br/noticia.php?id=8245>.

12. Youth detention centers totally inadequate. (1996, November 6). *SEJEP*, no. 251.

13. Ana Vasconcelos, the director of Casa da Passagem, a halfway house for street girls, said, "I am unable to comprehend why so many policemen have this fixation with kicking pregnant girls in the stomach."

14. Women can obtain legal abortions in Brazil only in the case of rape or incest, or to save the woman's life. About 30 per cent of all pregnancies end in abortion, despite these restrictive laws. Some doctors will perform abortions otherwise, but for a fee that is out of reach for most poor women. Nonetheless, 3.4 million abortions are performed each year. Twenty per cent result in infection, fatal in half the cases, totaling 400,000 abortion fatalities per year. The young girls I knew who got pregnant took Cictotec (misoprostol, a synthetic prostaglandin), an ulcer medicine sold over the counter, which induces uterine contractions. Then they would go to the emergency room to have a dilation and curettage for a "miscarriage." See Santos, C.F. (1981). Brazil: The health implications of urban pauperism. In P.W. Blair (Ed.), *Health needs of the world's poor women*. Washington: Equity Policy Center; *Latin America Regional Reports: Brazil* (1987, 17 September); Barroso, C. (1982). *Mulher, Sociedade, e Estado no Brasil*. São Paulo: Editora Brasiliense/UNICEF, p. 96.

CHAPTER SEVEN
CONCLUSION

The Brazilian Constitution (Article 227) states that "it is the duty of the family, society and state to assure children and adolescents, with absolute priority, of the rights to life, health, food, education, recreation, professional training, culture, dignity, respect, freedom, and family and community life, in addition to safeguarding them from all forms of neglect, discrimination, exploitation, violence, cruelty and oppression." Roberto da Silva, now 39 and an "ex" street kid, exercised this right by filing a court action against the state of São Paulo, holding the state responsible for the conditions that led to his living on the street.[1] For most of the poor families described here, conforming to these exigencies, without sufficient resources, is a wearisome challenge (Ennew, 1995).

There are a number of different approaches, some meeting with greater success than others, in addressing the issue of child labor, and poverty in general.

First, there are interventions that target individual children and their families. A number of programs have been initiated whose aim is to make children's labor dispensable by providing financial and other assistance to poor families, ultimately buoying school attendance. The results from these programs are encouraging; in the last 10 years, school attendance has increased, and child labor has declined in Brazil. The *Bolsa Escola* (school scholarship) is a conditional cash grant program started in 1996 that gives mothers approximately US$6 per month per child (ages 6–15, up to three children) as long as the children maintain 85 per cent attendance. The *Bolsa Família* (family scholarship) program supplements family income with a monthly stipend of about US$14 for families earning less than US$35 per month. The *Program for the Eradication of Child*

Labor (PETI) was launched in 1996 in the southern state of Mato Grosso do Sul. Until the 1990s, it targeted only those children in rural areas working in the most dangerous types of work, such as in the tobacco, sisal, and sugar cane plantations, charcoal kilns, brickyards, and mines. It provides R$40 for urban families and R$25 for rural families per child between the ages of 6 and 14. In Recife, however, the program's coverage at the end of the 1990s was only 2 per cent and had little effect on reducing child labor.[2] Some municipalities have given food or gas in lieu of cash payments (Levinas, Barbosa, & Tourinho, 2001, p. 8). Other irregularities included over 14,000 payments made to families with children over the age of 16.[3] Other programs include *Fome Zero* (Zero Hunger), created by President Lula[4] in 2003, and *Auxílio Gas* (gas voucher) programs. In some locations, lax monitoring and enforcement allows parents to collect subsidies even though their children are repeatedly absent from school. Others critique the proliferation of "*bolsas*" as unsustainable, and producing financial dependency in lieu of employment, but these comments are usually from those who do not depend on these types of subsidies to survive. Stable, waged jobs for adults would certainly contribute to the likelihood that children would spend more time in school.

Some schools provide children with a *cesta básica*. However a number of parents complain that the baskets contain foodstuffs of extremely poor quality, things they "would not even purchase for themselves if they had the money." Essential items such as toilet paper, sanitary napkins, toothbrushes, and toothpaste are not included.

The ABRINQ Foundation, an NGO started in 1990, promotes children's rights by engaging in advocacy, services, and monitoring of labor standards in the shoe, fruit, and sugar industries. Companies that comply with labor standards (no child labor was used in the making of its product) receive a "seal" from the organization.

Interventions that have been less successful are those whose primary goal is to reinsert a "lost" or "stolen" childhood, a notion based on an idealized image of family and home as nurturing environments underpinned by stable relationships. These are certainly well-intended efforts, but they rarely address the underlying conditions that generate and maintain poverty, or the consequences of the loss of children's earnings in the household. They tend to be remedial, psychologically based interventions that focus on "good parenting skills." These skills include inculcating the "value" of keeping children in school, recreation, and providing a nurturing home.

The goal of one US NGO in Recife was "family preservation."[5] However, staying with one's family does not quarantine one from danger or exploitation. Frankly, to remain in a household where one is unwanted is far from empowering. If children are pitied because they had their childhood stolen, perhaps they should not be pitied any more than their parents, who are living in the same "black holes" of "structural irrelevance" (Castells, 2000, pp. 165–68). It is in these vulnerable and precarious spaces where broad economic inequity, low wages, lack of access to education and health services, inadequate diets and malnutrition, disease, and crime become major if not prime factors in "family disintegration." Without social and economic reforms that link the poor to networks of information, wealth, and power, these black holes will produce "wasted children" (Castells, 2000, pp. 162–64) trapped in cycles of illiteracy, poverty, and social exclusion in jobs that are poorly remunerated and that have few transferable skills.[6]

It is important to note that significantly more children in Brazil die each year due to diseases related to poverty—diarrheal diseases and malnutrition—than from hazards associated with their work. In poor communities such as the ones described in Chapter 3, it borders on miraculous if adults are somehow able to shield their children from "growing up too fast" and missing out on a pampered and privileged childhood. These children are not buffered or sequestered from the "violence of everyday life" (Scheper-Hughes, 1992) or hidden in homes behind cement walls with barbed wire or shards of glass on top. The narratives of children I spoke to were rarely framed by an idealized norm of a pampered and privileged childhood, nor did they speak of being "robbed" of a childhood that was never possible for them. They are acutely conscious of the differences between themselves and wealthy kids, and envy those who do not have to work. Most hate the fact that they have to work, feel it is drudgery, and dream of a standard of living that will satisfy their consumer desires. Their priority is not to recapture a lost childhood, but to have some relief from the obligations, responsibilities, and risks of living in poverty. Without the economic restructuring that would lift people out of poverty, a protected and prolonged childhood seems unlikely (Boyden, 1990).

Open discussion on children's rights *as workers* is difficult because it nervously leans toward condoning the exploitation of children. Policies that would mandate benefits for child workers would effectively abolish the distinction between adult and child workers. Yet at a March 1997 meeting on child labor sponsored by the International Labor Organization (ILO), a number of children challenged the ILO representative during a panel discussion. While the sponsors advocated for the elimination of child labor, the children advocated for *transformation*, not abolishment. Policies that prohibit children from working in one arena usually mean they have to search for work somewhere else anyway. The children said they wanted better wages and hours, jobs with health and accident insurance, and unemployment compensation. Like other workers, they are tired and want paid leaves. They want vehicles for channeling grievances about their work, someone to complain to if people do not pay, or if they are harassed. They want to be recognized as laborers and expose exploitation. They want to be invited to conferences, and participate in the planning and policies that are made on their behalf (Johnson, Ivan-Smith, Gordon, Pridmore, & Scott, 1998; Guijt, Fuglesang, & Kisada, 1994; Hart, 1997).

One has to be cautious, however, about interpreting these demands as a reflection of children's strong "work ethic." The work ethic is a sociocultural construction, developed during the nineteenth century that refers to the *moral* value of work. It is a belief system that categorizes and juxtaposes poor people who work as "deserving" against those who do not work as "undeserving," shiftless, and lazy. The deserving poor accept any job, despite exploitation, risk, and lack of financial mobility, because "any job is more worthy than no job" (Katz, 1989). The discursive power of the notion of "having a work ethic," however, eschews the exploitative use of inexpensive (child) labor and normalizes structural violence by rendering their work "inevitable," even positive, while at the same time criticizing it as abusive by their parents.

The future for many of the world's poor children, and the poor in general, depends on the continued efforts of successful programs and interventions such as those mentioned above (see Appendix B for a list organizations that address these issues). Global processes will continue to reconfigure politics, power, markets, and forms of production and distributions of wealth. These in turn will affect children's lives and the nature and extent of their labor, how they express their discontent, and how they define themselves in the contemporary world. Shifts in the use of rural and urban spaces, transnational linkages, crime trends, and social movements will challenge the access to resources and shape the face of poverty.

It is therefore important to continue to listen to what children say as agents, whether it is in regard to the definition of research agendas or political regulation, rather than viewing them only as humble heroes or victims, and deciding a priori what is "in their best interests." How they see their work in relation to particular people, locations, and moments in time are fruitful arenas for documenting the changing nature of work and consumption. For example, what happens when these laborers age and often require the earnings of their own children? In the *sertão* (semi-arid rural interior) of Ceará, a number of youth I interviewed saw themselves as "on the move" rather than "tied to the land," revising or discarding altogether the relationship to rural life through labor. There is little for them to do, except to migrate or create networks with people living outside the area. In a *quilombo* (maroon community) in Paraíba, despite efforts by community members encouraging youth to connect to their "African" ancestry, young people wanted to leave the mountain, learn to use computers, learn foreign languages, and travel. They did not see "traditional" activities, such as making clay pots to sell, as economically viable or desirable. Despite stereotypes of being "rooted to the land," these contemporary youth covet jobs in the city and leave with no intention of returning.

Finally, we should all encourage public debate on child labor, the enforcement of standards and laws that protect children's rights, and mobilize with people from different segments of society in various parts of the world in promoting cultural and economic rights in order to alter the most egregious effects of structural violence.

NOTES

1. Former street-youth plans to sue state. (1996, 6 November). *SEJEP*, no. 251.
2. According to the UNICEF website, almost all of the children aged 7–14 living in the garbage dump mentioned in Chapter 4 are enrolled in school, with their families enrolled in the *bolsa escola* program.

3. PETI também atende adultos. (2005, June 10). *Jornal do Commercio*, p. 7.

4. Lula (Luis Inácio da Silva) was the worker's party candidate, a metalworker from a poor family in the Northeast. He was elected by a significant popular vote in 2003.

5. According to Gramsci, "even caring can be hegemonic." Gramsci, A. (1970). *The modern prince and other writings*. New York: International Publishers. In her study of Nepali children in refugee camps, Rachel Hinton (1990) emphasizes the disjuncture between donor-driven agendas (psychological counseling for trauma) and the priorities of the children and their families. Many women were puzzled with the emphasis by NGOs on rape as a distinct event, rather than the larger issue of loss of livelihood due to their refugee status, which to them had longer-term consequences for survival. Hinton, R. (1999). Seen but not heard: refugee children and models of intervention. In C. Panter-Brick & M.T. Smith (Eds.), *Abandoned children*. Cambridge: Cambridge University Press.

6. Departamento Intersindical de Estatística e Estudos Sócio-Econômicos [DIEESE]. (1997). O Trabalho Tolerado de Crianças até Catorze Anos. Accessed from <http://www.dieese.org.br>. Research was conducted in six capital cities (Belém, Recife, Goiânia, Belo Horizonte, São Paulo, and Porto Alegre) on education and work among children 7–14 years old.

APPENDIX A
SAMPLE SURVEY[1]

Demographics: age, sex, population; race/ethnicity

Local environment: layout, boundaries, topography, industry, schools, churches; social movements; police, gangs, drug use

Housing: type of house/land; number of rooms, material for construction; where people sleep, eat; material objects (owned, borrowed, repaired); differences between homes in same community; water source; type of electricity, sanitation, and garbage disposal; rent, own, squatter

Local economy: paid/unpaid work; occupations, level of unemployment, income, migration; prostitution, hustling, begging; prices, credit, savings; property, income/educational levels; mortality/morbidity rates; health care and social services; contraceptive use

Family and household: kinship chart, types of unions, adoption; migration, community of origin; life histories: critical transition points (illness, injury, drug/alcohol problems, migration, birth, death, abandonment, marriage/divorce, school, job loss); occupation, education of household members

Formal schooling: when began/left; experience of school; working and school

Employment: different ways for earning, how long, how they access jobs, learn jobs; number of hours/day they work; how much they earn per day/week/month; how much money kept for oneself/given to household; decision making: who decides how the money is spent at home; how much money spent on: food, clothing, health care, rent, transportation, school, alcohol, drugs, and debts; non-remunerated work; aspirations, expectations, preferences, strategies

NOTE

1. Some of these variables are taken from household studies conducted by Nieuwenhuys (1994), Wallerstein (1984), and Friedman (1984).

APPENDIX B
ORGANIZATIONS THAT ADDRESS THE ISSUE OF CHILD LABOR

In Brazil, there are hundreds of foundations, non-governmental organizations, and federal, state, and local organizations that provide funding, technical assistance, research, and direct services to youth. Projects are aimed at citizenship and human rights; economic development, poverty eradication, income generation; heath and education; and the media. Although some of the smaller, less well-funded organizations may not have web sites, contact information is usually available through links on the web sites of funding agencies or through a "Google" search. Many welcome volunteer participation. Most of the larger, international agencies (ILO) provide on-line research reports, documents, and links to projects in Brazil.

> *ABRINQ foundation*
> http://www.fundabrinq.org.br
> An NGO founded in 1990 that focuses on actualizing the *Child and Adolescent Rights Act* (1990). They provide support for the development of libraries and literacy, curriculum materials, technology, professional development, and credit and financing for youth-managed businesses, projects, and programs. They also provide a "seal of approval" to businesses that follow the "10 commitments" of good business. These include not violating child labor laws; providing on-site child care; encouraging workers to keep children under 18 in school; providing incentives for pregnant women to get prenatal care; providing space for women to breastfeed their children up to six months; encouraging workers to register their children (birth certificates); and investing a percentage of profits in child-oriented projects.

Afro Reggae Cultural Group (Grupo Cultural AfroReggae—GCAR)
http://www.afroreggae.org.br
Formed in 1993, the group targets young people interested in reggae, soul, and hip-hop. They run workshops in music and the arts, soccer, recycling, literacy, IT, filmmaking, and domestic violence. They have a newspaper and radio program; provide social assistance to the elderly, *cesta básicas*, and health information and education. The evolution of the organization, its musicians, and mission are the subject of the film *Favela Rising.*

Association of Paper, Carton, and Recyclable Material Pickers (Asmare)
http://www.asmare.org.br
Founded by Dona Geralda in 1990, herself a former *catadora* (garbage picker), and made up of *catadores* (garbage pickers), association members receive technical training on recycling and environmental laws, legal assistance, medical and dental support, life insurance, micro-credit for housing construction, and dividends. They have developed links with companies and schools; they also run a pharmacy and a market. They have a "Cultural House" with a café, stage, art gallery, and store, which sells products made from scavenged materials.

Brazil Foundation
http://www.brazilfoundation.org
Funds projects in education, health, human rights, citizenship, and culture.

Brazilian Community Action/Ação Comunitária do Brasil (ACB)
http://www.acaocomunitaria.org.br/home/index.asp
Provides training programs to create small business ventures and employment for local, low-income youth.

Casa de Passagem
http://www.casadepassagem.org.br
Support network for children at risk; research, outreach, and educational projects.

Centro Cultural Aldeia do Monte
Founded in 2003 by Fofão (featured in this book) with his wife Maria, this NGO, located in the heart of Monte, a local community in Olinda, focuses on teaching dance, music, and theater to children in the community.

Centro de Cultura Luis Freire
http://www.cclf.org.br
Outreach and workshops on democracy and human rights, poverty, education and culture; public policy and leadership training.

Fundação Casa Grande Memorial do Homem Kariri
Called the "Kids' School of the Sertão," the foundation trains youth in music, radio, theater, television and video production, as well as publishing, arts management, and IT. The children have created a museum, community radio program, magazines, books, and videos, targeting children in the semi-arid *sertão*.

International Labor Organization (ILO)
http://www.ilo.org
The ILO is involved in worldwide research, policy, and technical support on child labor. The headquarters is located in Geneva, and they have a worldwide network of regional and national offices.

Living Wheel/Roda Viva
http://www.rodaviva.org.br
Focuses on children's rights by "connecting the spokes to the center." Builds partnerships among local government, businesses, community organizations, the church, and the media to evaluate and address local issues.

Movimento Nacional dos Meninos e Meninas de Rua
http://www.mnmmr.org.br
The National Movement of Street Youth (MNMMR) is an NGO that works on behalf of children's rights. They are engaged in advocacy, outreach, workshops, and policy.

Projeto Axé

http://www.projetoaxe.org.br

The Axe Project is an NGO founded in 1990 that targets children living in the street, working children, and their families through education and outreach, cultural activities, advocacy, and professional training.

Projeto Renascer

http://www.prorenascer.com.br/indexenglish.html

Provides tutoring, literacy, and income-generating programs for children in the community. Volunteers welcome.

UNICEF (United Nations Children's Fund)

http://www.unicef.org/brazil

Provides financial support and technical training for projects that invest in children's rights; the development of educational, health, and cultural projects; infrastructure; and evaluation.

Viva Rio

http://www.vivario.org.br

A comprehensive non-profit organization that provides assistance, training, opportunities, tutoring, and educational extension workshops; legal assistance; and media services, as well as promoting disarmament and cultural activities for those in poor communities mainly in Rio, but they also have projects in the Northeast of the country. They also have a well-organized volunteer/intern program that accepts candidates from outside Brazil.

REFERENCES

Abrúcio, F. (2000). Beyond mere discomfort: How to attack corruption. Retrieved August 26 from <http://www.Infobrazil.com>.

Albuquerque, D.M. de., Jr. (1999). *A invencão do Nordeste e outras artes*. Recife: Fundação Joaquim Nabuco; São Paulo: Massangana/Cortez.

Andrade, J. (2006, July 8). Racismo de revestrés. [editorial] *Jornal do Commercio*, 15.

Andrews, G.R. (1991). *Blacks and whites in São Paulo, Brazil, 1888–1988*. Madison: University of Wisconsin Press.

Appadurai, Arjun. (1996). *Modernity at large: Cultural dimensions of globalization*. Minneapolis: University of Minnesota Press.

Aragão e Frota, L.S. De. (1984) *Documentaçao oral e a temática da seca* (Estudos). Brasília: Senado Federal.

Araújo, T.B. de. (2004). Northeast, northeasts: What northeast? *Latin American Perspectives*, 31(2), 16–41.

Ariès, P. (1962). *Centuries of childhood: A social history of family life* (R. Baldick, Trans.). London: Cape.

Association of Farmworker Opportunity Programs. (2005). *Children in the fields: The inequitable treatment of child farm workers*. Retrieved November 18, 2005 from <http://www.afop.org/child_labor/>.

Azevedo, T. de. (1975). *Democrácia racial: Ideologia e realidade*. Petrópolis, Rio de Janeiro: Editora Vozes.

Banks, I. (2000). *Hair matters*. New York: New York University Press.

Bastide, R., & Fernandes, F. (1971[1959]). *Brancos e negros em São Paulo* (3rd ed.). São Paulo: Campanhia Editora Nacional.

Benería, L. (2003). *Gender, development and globalization: Economics as if all people mattered*. New York: Routledge.

Berliner, D. (2005). An impossible transmission: Youth religious memories in Guinea-Conakry. *American Ethnologist*, 32(4), 576–92.

Berquó, E. (1999). Sterilization and race in São Paulo. In R. Reichmann (Ed.), *Race in contemporary Brazil: From indifference to equality.* University Park: Pennsylvania State University Press.

Beserra, B. (2004). Introduction. *Latin American Perspectives, 31*(2), 3–15.

Blackwood, E. (2005). Wedding bell blues: Marriage, missing men, and matrifocal follies. *American Ethnologist, 32*(1), 3–19.

Blake, A., Arbache, J.S., Teles, V., & Sinclair, T. (2005). Tourism and poverty alleviation in Brazil. http://www.un.br./cet/noticias/Adam_Blake. pdf>. Accessed November 25, 2006.

Blake, S.E. (2003). The medicalization of nordestinos: Public health and regional identity and northeastern Brazil, 1889–1930. *The Americas, 60*(2), 217–48.

Body-Bendrot, S. (2000). *The social control of cities: A comparative perspective.* Oxford: Blackwell.

Borges, D.E. (1992). *The family in Bahia, Brazil: 1870–1945.* Stanford: Stanford University Press.

Boswell, J. (1988). *The kindness of strangers: The abandonment of children in Western Europe from late antiquity to the Renaissance.* Harmondsworth: Penguin.

Bourdieu, P. (1984). *Distinction: A social critique of the judgment of taste.* (R. Nice, Trans.). Cambridge, MA: Harvard University Press.

Boutet de Monvel, A. (1963). *Introduction to Rousseau.* London: Dent.

Boyden, J. (1990). Childhood and the policy makers: A comparative perspective on the globalization of childhood. In A. James & A. Prout (Eds.), *Constructing and reconstructing childhood: Contemporary issues in the sociological study of childhood* (pp. 184–215). London: Falmer Press.

Brazil arrests 11 for organ trafficking. (2003, December 4). *Toronto Star.*

Buckley, S. (2000, March 16). The littlest laborers: Why does child labor continue to thrive in the developing world? *The Washington Post,* A1.

Caetano, A.J. (2000). *Sterilization for votes in the Brazilian Northeast: The case of Pernambuco.* Unpublished doctoral dissertation, University of Texas, Austin.

Caldeira, T. (1992). *City of walls: Crime, segregation, and citizenship in São Paulo.* Berkeley: University of California Press.

Cardoso, F.H. (1962). *Capitalismo e escravidão no Brasil meridional.* São Paulo: Difusão Europeia do Livro.

Carvalho, J.M. de. (1992). Brazil (1870–1914): The force of tradition. *Journal of Latin American Studies*, 24(Supplement), 145–62.

Castells, M. (2000). *End of millennium*. Oxford: Blackwell.

Castro, J. de. 1952. *Geography of hunger*. Boston: Little Brown.

Centro Josué de Castro. (1992/93). *Os trabalhadores invisíveis: Crianças e adolescentes dos Canaviais de Pernambuco*. Recife: Centro Josué de Castro, Estudos e Pesquisas (Org.).

Chalhoub, S. (1993). The politics of disease control: Yellow fever and race in nineteenth century Rio de Janeiro. *Journal of Latin American Studies*, 25(3), 441–63.

Chalhoub, S. (1996). *Cidade febril: Cortiços e epidemias na corte imperial*. São Paulo: Companhia das Letras.

Child and Adolescent Rights Act. (1990). O Ministerio Publico do Trabalho na Erradicaçao do Trabalho Infantil e na Proteçao do Trabalho do Adolescente. Retrieved from <www.pgt.mpt.gov.br/trabinfantil/atuacao.html>.

Clifford, J. & Marcus, G.E. (Eds.) (1986). *Writing culture: The poetics and politics of ethnography*. Berkeley: University of California Press.

Cole, T. (1999). *Selling the Holocaust from Auschwitz to Schindler: How history is bought, packaged and sold*. New York: Routledge.

Crick, M. (1996). Representations of international tourism in the social sciences: Sun, sex, sights, saving and servility. In Y. Apostolopoulos, S. Leivadi, & A. Yiannakis (Eds.), *The sociology of tourism: Theoretical and empirical investigations*. London: Routledge.

Cunha, E. da. (1944). *Rebellion in the back lands* (Samuel Putnam, Trans. 1902 Os Sertões: campanha de Canudos). Chicago: University of Chicago Press.

Da Matta, R. (1995). On the Brazilian urban poor: An anthropological report (C. Dunn, Trans.), *Democracy and social policy series* (Working Paper No. 10). Notre Dame, IN: Kellogg Institute and CEBRAP.

Davin, A. (1982). Child labour, the working-class family, and domestic ideology in 19th century Britain. *Development and Change*, 13(4), 663–52.

Degler, C. (1971). *Neither Black nor white: Slavery and race relations in Brazil and the United States*. New York: Macmillan.

deMause, L. (1974). *The history of childhood*. New York: Psychohistory Press.

DIEESE [Departamento Intersindical de Estatística e Estudos Sócio-Econômicos]. (2005). O Trabalho Tolerado de Crianças até Catorze Anos. Retrieved October 2006 from <http://www.diesse.com.br>.

Dimenstein, G. (1991). *Brazil: War on children*. London: Latin America Bureau.

Domingos, M. (2004). The powerful in the outback of the Brazilian Northeast. *Latin American Perspectives*, *31*(2), 94–111.

Donzelot, J. (1986). *The policing of families*. London: Hutchinson.

Douglas, M. (1966). *Purity and danger: An analysis of the concepts of pollution and taboo*. London: Ark.

Douglas, M. (1994). *Risk and blame: Essays in cultural theory*. London: Routledge.

Edelman, M., & Haugerud, A. (2005). *The anthropology of development and globalization*. Oxford: Blackwell.

Ennew, J. (1985). *Juvenile streetworkers in Lima, Peru*. London: Overseas Development Administration.

Ennew, J. (1995). Outside childhood: Street children's rights. In B. Franklin (Ed.), *The handbook of children's rights: Comparative policy and practice* (pp. 201–14). New York: Routledge.

Falcão, Rosa. (2006, July 1). Precarização mais próxima. *Diario de Pernambuco*, p. B8.

Family Health International [FHI]. (2004). *Brazil: Consequences of tubal ligation for women's lives*. Retrieved December 2005 from <http://www.fhi.org/en/RH/Pubs/wsp/fctshts/Brazil2.htm>.

Fischer, M.M.J. (2003). *Emergent forms of life and the anthropological voice*. Durham, NC: Duke University Press.

Folbre, N. (1986). Hearts and spades: Paradigms of household economics. *World Development*, *14*(2), 245–55.

Fontaine, P.M. (1980). Research in the political economy of Afro-Latin America. *Latin American Research Review*, *15*(2), 111–41.

Freyre, G. (1946). *The masters and the slaves: A study in the development of Brazilian civilization*. New York: Knopf.

Friedman, K. (1984). Households as income pooling units. In J. Smith, I. Wallerstein, & H.D. Evers (Eds.), *Households and the world economy* (pp. 37–55). Thousand Oaks, CA: Sage.

GELEDÉS, Instituto da Mulher Negra. (1991). *Esterilização: Impunidade ou regulamentação?* São Paulo: GELEDÉS.

Gill, I.S., Montenegro, C.E., & Dömeland, D. (Eds.). (2002). *Crafting labor policy: Techniques and lessons from Latin America*. The International Bank for Reconstruction and Development/World Bank and New York: Oxford University Press.

Goldani, A.M. (2001, August). *Rethinking Brazilian fertility decline.* Paper presented at the XXIV General Population Conference, International Union for the Scientific Study of Population, Salvador, Bahia, Brazil.

Goldin, C. (1981). Family strategies and the family economy in the late nineteenth century: The role of secondary workers. In T. Hershberg (Ed.), *Philadelphia: Work, space, family and experience in the nineteenth century* (pp. 277–310). New York: Oxford University Press.

Gonzales de la Rocha, M. (1995). The urban family and poverty in Latin America. *Latin American Perspectives, 85*(22), 12–31.

Gordillo, G. (2002). The breath of devils: Memories and places of an experience of terror. *American Ethnologist, 29*(1), 33–57.

Gramsci, A. (1971). *Selections from the prison notebooks* (Q. Hoare & G.N. Smith, Eds. & Trans.). London: Lawrence and Wishart.

Griffen, P., & Edwards, A.C. (1993). Rates of return to education in Brazil: Do labor market conditions matter? *Economics of Education Review, 12*(3), 245–56.

Grootaert, C., & Kanbur, R. (1995). Child labor: An economic perspective. *International Labor Review, 134*(2), 187–203.

Guijt, I., Fuglesang, A., & Kisada, Y. (Eds.). (1994). *It is the young trees that make a thick forest: A report on Redd Barna's learning experiences with participatory rural appraisal in Kyakatebe, Uganda.* Stevenage, UK: United Nations Environment Program, Earthprint.

Guimarães Sá, I. dos. (2000). Circulation of children in eighteenth-century Portugal. In C. Panter-Brick & M.T. Smith (Eds.), *Abandoned children* (pp. 27–40). Cambridge: Cambridge University Press.

Haines, M. (1981). Poverty, economic stress, and family in a late nineteenth-century American city: Whites in Philadelphia, 1880. In T. Hershberg (Ed.), *Philadelphia* (pp. 240–76). New York: Oxford University Press.

Hamilton, W., & Azevedo, N. (1999). A febre amarela no Brasil: memória de um medico da Fundação Rockefeller. *História, Ciências, Saúde: Manguinhos, 5*(3), 733–54.

Hareven, T. (1991). Synchronizing individual time, family time, and historical time. In J. Bender & D. Wellbery (Eds.), *Chronotypes: The construction of time* (pp. 167–82). Stanford, CA: Stanford University Press.

Harris, M., & Ross, E. (Eds.). (1987). *Death, sex and fertility: Population regulation in preindustrial and developing societies.* New York: Columbia University Press.

Harris, O. (1984). Households as natural units. In K. Young, C. Wolkowitz, & R. McCullagh (Eds.), *Marriage and the market* (2nd ed., pp. 136–55). London: Routledge and Kegan Paul.

Hart, K. (1973). Informal income opportunities and urban employment in Ghana. *Journal of Modern African Studies, 11*, 61–89.

Hart, R. (1997). *Children's participation: The theory and practice of involving young citizens in community development and environmental care.* London: UNICEF Earthscan Publications.

Harvey, D. (1989). *The condition of postmodernity: An enquiry into the origins of cultural change.* Cambridge, MA: Blackwell.

Harvey, D. (2000). *Spaces of hope.* Berkeley: University of California Press.

Hasenbalg, C. (1979). *Discriminação e desigualdades raciais no Brasil.* Rio de Janeiro: Graal.

Hawes, J., & Hiner, N.R. (1991). *Children in historical and comparative perspective.* Westport, CT: Greenwood Press.

Hecht, T. (1998). *At home in the street.* Cambridge: Cambridge University Press.

Hendrick, H. (1990). Constructions and reconstructions of British childhood: An interpretative survey, 1800 to the present. In A. James & A. Prout (Eds.), *Constructing and reconstructing childhood* (pp. 35–59). New York: Falmer.

Hinchberger, B. (2005). *Community tourism helps fishing village keep speculators at bay.* Americas Program of the International Relations Center (IRC). Retrieved December 2005 from <www.irc-one.org>.

Hoghughi, M. (1983). *The delinquent: Directions for social control.* London: Burnett.

Huggins, M.K., & Macturk, J. (2000). *Armed and dangerous.* Retrieved from the Resource Center of the Americas, <http:www.Americas.org>.

Ianni, O. (1962). *As metamorfoses do escravo.* São Paulo: Difusão Europeia do Livro.

Ianni, O. (1972). *Raças e classes sociais no Brasil* (2nd ed.). São Paulo: Editora Civilização Brasileira.

Ianni, O. (1978). *Escravidão e racismo.* São Paulo: HUCITEC.

Ignatieff, M. (1998). Is nothing sacred? The ethics of television. *The warrior's honour: Ethnic war and the modern conscience.* London: Chatto and Windus.

Jackson, D.K. (1994). Three glad races: Primitivism and ethnicity in Brazilian modernist literature. *Modernism/modernity, 1*(2), 89–112.

Jenks, C. (1998). *Childhood.* New York: Routledge.

Jesus, C.M. de. (1962). *Child of the dark.* New York: Dutton.

Johnson, V., Ivan-Smith, E., Gordon, G., Pridmore, P., & Scott, P. (1998). *Stepping forward: Children and young people's participation in the development process.* London: Intermediate Technology Publication.

Katz, M.B. (1989). *The undeserving poor: From the war on poverty to the war on welfare.* New York: Pantheon.

Kertzer, D. (2000). The lives of foundlings in Italy. In C. Panter-Brick & M.T. Smith (Eds.), *Abandoned children* (pp. 41–56). Cambridge: Cambridge University Press.

Kleinman, A., Das, V., & Lock, M. (1997). *Social suffering.* Berkeley: University of California Press.

Kundera, M. (1980). *The book of laughter and forgetting* (M.H. Heim, Trans.). New York: Knopf.

La Fontaine, J. (1986). An anthropological perspective on children in social worlds. In M. Richards & P. Light (Eds.), *Children of social worlds: Development in a social context* (pp. 10–30). Cambridge: Polity.

Langer, L. (1982). *Versions of survival: The Holocaust and the human spirit.* Albany: State University of New York Press.

Laslett, P., & Wall, R. (1972). *Household and family in past times.* Cambridge: Cambridge University Press.

Leu, L. (2004). The press and the spectacle of violence in contemporary Rio de Janeiro. *Journal of Latin American Cultural Studies, 13,* 343–55.

Levinas, L., Barbosa, L., & Tourinho, O. (2001). *Assessing local minimum income programs in Brazil.* Geneva: ILO.

Levine, R.M. (1998). *Father of the poor: Vargas and his era.* Cambridge: Cambridge University Press.

Levison, D., Anker, R., Ashraf, S., & Barge, S. (1998). Is child labour really necessary in India's carpet industry? In R. Anker, S. Barge, S. Rajagopal, & M.P. Joseph (Eds.), *Economics of child labour in hazardous industries of India.* Baroda: Centre for Operations Research and Training.

Lewis, J. (1986). Anxieties about the family and the relationships between parents, children, and the state in twentieth century England. In M. Richards & P. Light (Eds.), *Children of social worlds* (pp. 31–54). Cambridge: Polity Press.

Lewis, O. (1966a). *La Vida: A Puerto Rican family in the culture of poverty, San Juan and New York.* New York: Random House.

Lewis, O. (1966b). The culture of poverty. *Scientific American, 215*(4), 19–25.

Lomnitz, L. (1988). The social and economic organization of a Mexican shanty town. In J. Gugler (Ed.), *The urbanization of the Third World* (pp. 242–63). Oxford: Oxford University Press.

Lovell, N. (1998). Introduction. In N. Lovell (Ed.), *Locality and belonging* (pp. 1–24). London: Routledge.

Löwy, I. (1997). What/who should be controlled? Opposition to yellow fever campaigns in Brazil, 1900–39. In A. Cunningham & B. Andrews (Eds.), *Western medicine as contested knowledge* (pp. 124–46). New York: St. Martin's Press.

Löwy, I. (1999). Representação e intervenção em saúde pública: virus, mosquitos e especialistas da Fundação Rockefeller no Brasil. *História, Ciências, Saúde: Manguinhos, 5*(3) (Nov 1998/Feb.1999), 647–77.

Maio, M.C. & Santos, R.V. (2005). Política de cotas Raciais, os "Olhos da Sociedade" e os usos da antropologia: O caso do vestibular da universidade de Brasília (UNB). *Horizontes Antropológicos, 11*(23), 181–214.

Mamede, M.A.B. (1996). *A construção do Nordeste pela média*. Fortaleza: Secult.

Menezes, M.A. de. (2004). Migration patterns of Paraíba peasants. *Latin American Perspectives, 31*(2), 112–34.

Ministry of Culture. (2006). *Living culture. National culture, education and citizenship program.*

Mugnaini, A. (2006). Música Sertaneja: What it is—and isn't. Retrieved May 26, 2006 from <http://www.brazilmax.com/pff.cfm/tborigem/fe_music/id/9>.

Nascimento, A. do. (1978). *O genocídio do negro brasileiro-um processo de racismo mascarado*. Rio de Janeiro: Paz e Terra.

Nascimento, A. do. (1991). *O quilombismo. Carta: Falas, relexões, memórias.* Infome. Brasília, Gabinete do Senador Darcy Ribeiro, pp. 21–26.

Neiva, A., & Penna, B. (1916). Viagem cientifica pelonorte da Bahia, sudoeste de Pernambuco, sul do Piauhí e de norte a sul de Goiaz. *Memorias do Institute Oswaldo Cruz*, 8(3), 74–224.

Neves, F. de Castro. (1998). Economia Moral versus Moral Economia (Ou: O Que é economicamente correto para os Pobres?). *Projeto História, 16,* 39–57.

Neves, F. de Castro. (2000). *A multidão e a história: Saques e outras ações de massas no Ceará*. Rio de Janeiro: Relume Dumará.

Nicholas, D. (1995). Child and adolescent labor in the late medieval city: A Flemish model in regional perspective. *English Historical Review, 110,* 1103–31.

Nieuwenhuys, O. (1994). *Children's lifeworlds: Gender, welfare and labor in the developing world.* New York: Routledge.

Nobles, M. (2000). *Shades of citizenship.* Stanford: Stanford University Press.

Nogueira, O. (1955). Preconceito de marca e preconceito racial de origem. *Anais do XXXI Congresso Internatcaionl de Americanistas, 1,* 409–34. São Paulo: Ed. Anhembi.

Nogueira, S. (2004). A Cultura Material no processo educativo: Museus, objectos e ofícios tradicionais na reconstrução de identidades e evocação de memórias. *Os Urbanitas, 1*(2). Retrieved December 5, 2005 from <http://www.osurbanitas.org/>.

Oliveira e Oliveira, Eduardo de. (1974). Mulato, um obstáculo epistemológico. *Argumento, 1*(3): 65-73.

Pearse, A. (1961). Some characteristics of urbanization in the city of Rio de Janeiro. In P. Hauser (Ed.), *Urbanization in Latin America* (pp. 191–205). New York: UNESCO.

Pereira Lima, Paulo *Sem Fronteiras* (1997, December).

Perlman, J. (1976). *The myth of marginality.* Berkeley: University of California Press.

Pierson, D. (1967). *Negroes in Brazil: A study of race contact at Bahia.* Carbondale/Edwardsville: Southern Illinois University Press.

Pinheiro, P.S. (1996). Democracies without citizenship. *NACLA Report on the Americas, 30*(2), 17-42.

Pino, J.C. (1997). *Family and favela: The reproduction of poverty in Rio de Janeiro.* Westport, CT: Greenwood.

Platt, K. (1996). Places of experience and the experience of place. In L.S. Rouner (Ed.), *The longing for home* (pp. 112–27). Notre Dame, IN: University of Indiana.

Pollock, L. (1983). *Forgotten children: Parent-child relations from 1500 to 1800.* New York: Cambridge University Press.

Pollock, L. (1987). *A lasting relationship: Parents and children over three centuries.* Hanover, NH: University Press of New England.

Pontes, F., & Schmidt, S. (2001, January 28). A invasão silenciosa das favelas: Censo do IBGE revela que surgiu uma ocupação por mês na última década. *O Globo.*

Potter, J.E. (1999). The persistence of outmoded contraceptive regimes: The cases of Mexico and Brazil. *Population Development Review, 25*(4), 703–39.

Prado, R.M. (2003). As espécies Exóticas somos nós: Reflexão a propósito do ecoturismo na ilha grande. *Horizontes Antropológicos, 9*(20), 205-24.

Ribeiro, D. (2000). *The Brazilian people: Formation and meaning of Brazil.* Gainesville: University Press of Florida.

Rizzini, I., Muñoz-Vargas, M., & Galeano, L. (1992). *Childhood and urban poverty in Brazil: Street and working children and their families.* Florence: Innocenti Occasional Papers (Urban Child Series, No. 3).

Rizzini, I., & Rizzini, I. (1991). Menores Institucionalizados e Meninos de Rua: As Grandes Temas de Pesquisa na Decada de 80. In A. Fausto & R. Cervini (Eds.), *O trabalho e a Rua: Crianças e adolescentes no Brasil urbano dos anos 80.* São Paulo: Cortez Editora.

Rizzini, I., Rizzini, I., & Borges, F.R. (1998). Brazil: Children's strength is not in their work. In M.C. Salazar & W.A. Glasinovich (Eds.), *Child work and education: Five case studies from Latin America.* Florence: UNICEF.

Rizzini, I., Rizzini, I., Muñoz-Vargas, M., & Galeano, L. (1994). Brazil: A new concept of childhood. In C. Szanton-Blanc (Ed.), *Urban children in distress: Global predicaments and innovative strategies* (pp. 55–99). Florence: UNICEF/International Child Development Centre.

Robertson, P. (1974). Home as a nest: Middle class childhood in nineteenth century Europe. In L. deMause (Ed.), *The history of childhood* (pp. 407–31). New York: Psychohistory Press.

Rodgers, G., & Standing, G. (Eds.). (1981). *Child work, poverty, and underdevelopment.* Geneva: International Labor Office.

Rohter, L. (2004, May 23). Tracking the sale of a kidney on a path of poverty and hope. *New York Times.* Retrieved May 23, 2004 from <http://www.nytimes.com/2004/05/23/international/americas>.

Rojek, C. (1993). *Ways of escape: Modern transformations in leisure and travel.* London: Macmillan.

Rosemberg, F., & Andrade, L.F. (1999). Ruthless rhetoric: Child and youth prostitution in Brazil. *Childhood, 6*(1), 113–31.

Safa, H. (1999). Women coping with crisis: Social consequences of export-led industrialization in the Dominican Republic. *The North-South Agenda Papers* (No. 36). Coral Gables, FL: North-South Center, University of Miami.

Sansone, L. (2003). *Blackness without ethnicity: Constructing race in Brazil.* New York: Palgrave Macmillan.

Santos, M.S. dos. (2005, March). Representations of Black people in Brazilian museums. *Museum and Society, 3*(1), 51–65.

Scheper-Hughes, N. (1992). *Death without weeping: The violence of everyday life in Brazil.* Berkeley: University of California Press.

Scheper-Hughes, N. (1996a). Small wars and invisible genocides. *Social Science and Medicine, 43*(5), 889–900.

Scheper-Hughes, N. (1996b). Theft of life: Globalization of organ stealing rumors. *Anthropology Today, 12*(3), 3–11.

Scheper-Hughes, N. (2000). The global traffic in human organs. *Current Anthropology, 41*(2), 191–224.

Scheper-Hughes, N., & Hoffman, D. (1994). Kids out of place. *NECLAS Report on the Americas* (May/June).

Scheper-Hughes, N. & Hoffman, D. (1998). Brazilian apartheid: Street kids and the struggle for urban space. In N. Scheper-Hughes & C. Sargent (Eds.), *Small wars: The cultural politics of childhood* (pp. 352–88). Berkeley: University of California Press.

Schildkrout, E. (1981). The employment of children in Kano, Nigeria. In G. Rodgers & G. Standing (Eds.), *Child work, poverty and underdevelopment* (pp. 81–112). Geneva: International Labor Office.

Schwartzman, S. (2004). *As causas da pobreza.* Rio de Janeiro: Fundação Getúlio Vargas.

Servico Brasileiro de Justice e Paz [SEJUP]. (1995, March 30). No. 172. Retrieved March 30, 1995 from <http://www.oneworld.org/sejup/>.

Silva, B. da. (1997). *Benedita da Silva: An Afro-Brazilian woman's story of politics and love.* Oakland, CA: Food First Books.

Silva, Nelson doValle. (1985). Updating the cost of not being white in Brazil. In Pierre Michel Fontaine (Ed.), *Race, class and power in Brazil* (pp. 42-55). Berkeley: University of California Press.

Skidmore, T. (1983). Race and class in Brazil: Historical perspectives. *Luso-Brazilian Review, 20*(1), 104–18.

Slob, B., & Wilde, J. (2006). Tourism and sustainability in Brazil. The tourism value chain in Porto de Galinhas, Northeast Brazil. SOMO-Centre for Research on Multinational Corporations. <http://www.somo.nl>. Accessed November 25, 2006.

Smelser, N. (1959). *Social change and the Industrial Revolution*. Chicago: University of Chicago Press.

Soares, G., & Borges, D. (2004). A cor da morte. *Ciência Hoje, 35*(209), 26–31.

Sonhos de Verão. (1995, 18 January). *Isto É*, 38–44.

Soper, F.L., Rickard, E.R., & Crawford, P.J. (1934). The routine post-mortem removal of liver tissue from rapidly fatal fever cases for the discovery of silent yellow fever foci. *The American Journal of Hygiene, 19*(3), 549–66.

Sorj, B. (2005). *Civil societies north-north relations: NGOs and dependency* (Working paper No. 1). Rio de Janeiro: The Edelstein Center for Social Research.

Sousa Rios, K. (2001). *Campos de Concentração no Ceará: Isolamento e poder na Seca de 1932*. Fortaleza: Museu do Ceará.

Souza Martins, J. de. (1994). *O poder do atraso: Ensaios de sociologia da história lenta*. São Paulo: HUCITEC.

Spielberg, E. (1997). The myth of nimble fingers. In A. Ross (Ed.), *No sweat: Fashion, free trade and the rights of garment workers* (pp. 113–22). New York: Verso.

Stack, C. (1974). *All our kin*. New York: Harper and Row.

Steedman, C. (1991). *Childhood, culture and class in Britain: Margaret Macmillan 1860–1931*. London: Virago.

Stephens, S. (1995). Children and the politics of culture in late capitalism. In S. Stephens (Ed.), *Children and the Politics of Culture* (pp. 3–48).

Suor dos pequenos. VEJA (1995, August 31). 70-80.

Susser, I. (1996). The construction of poverty and homelessness in US cities. *Annual Review Anthropology, 25,* 411–35.

Sutton, A. (1994). *Slavery in Brazil*. London: Anti-Slavery International.

Szanton-Blanc, C. (1994). *Urban children in distress: Global predicaments and innovative strategies*. Langhorne, PA: Gorden and Breach.

Tannenbaum, F. (1946). *Slave and citizen: The Negro in the Americas*. New York: Vintage Books.

Tilly, L., & Scott, J. (Eds.). (1987). *Women, work, and family*. New York: Metheun.

Turner, P. (1993). *I heard it through the grapevine: Rumor in African-American culture*. Berkeley: University of California Press.

US Department of Labor [USDOL]. (2002). *Advancing the campaign against child labor: Efforts at the country level*. Washington, DC: Bureau of

International Labor Affairs. Retrieved December 2005 from <http://www.dol.gov/ILAB/reports/pubs_reports_ilab.htm>.

Vasconcelos, A. (1992, June 29–July 1). *Meninas e nulheres das ruas e da vida/ Prevenção a AIDS.* Paper presented at the Women and AIDS conference, State University of Rio de Janeiro, Institute of Social Medicine, Brazil.

Venâncio, R.P. (1999). *Famílias abandonadeas: assistência à criança de camadas populares no Rio de Janeiro e em Salvador, séculos XVIII e XIX.* Campinas: Papirus.

Villa, M.A. (2000). *Vida e morte no sertão: História das secas no Nordeste nos sécas no Nordeste nos séculos XIX e XX.* Editora Ática.

Wade, P. (1995). The cultural politics of blackness in Colombia. *American Ethnologist, 22*(2), 341–57.

Wagley, C. (1969). From caste to class in North Brazil. In M. Tumin (Ed.), *Comparative perspectives in race relations* (pp. 47–62). Boston: Little, Brown & Co.

Wallerstein, I.M. (1984). Household structures and labor-force formation in the capitalist world-economy. In J. Smith, I.M. Wallerstein, & H.D. Evers (Eds.), *Households and the world economy* (pp. 17–22). Thousand Oaks, CA: Sage.

Whitehead, A. (1984). "I'm hungry, mum": The politics of domestic budgeting. In K. Young, C. Wolkowitz, and R. McCullagh (Eds.), *Of marriage and the market: Women's subordination internationally and its lessons* (pp. 93–116). London: Routledge and Kegan Paul.

Wilk, R., & Miller, S. (1997). Some methodological issues in counting communities and households. *Human Organization, 56*(1), 64–70.

Wolf, E., & Hansen, E.C. (1972). *The human condition in Latin America.* New York: Oxford University Press.

Wolford, W. (2004). Of land and labor: Agrarian reform on the sugarcane plantations in northeast Brazil. *Latin American Perspectives, 31*(2), 147–70.

World Bank. (2005). World Country Brief: Brazil. Retrieved April 2005 from <www.worldbank.org>.

World Travel and Tourism Council. <http://www.wttc.org/TSA%202007/Executive%20Summary%202007.pdf>. Accessed March 28, 2007.

Young, Mei Ling. (1986). Analyzing household histories. In E. Berquó & P. Xenos (Eds.), *Family systems and cultural change* (pp. 176–200). Oxford: Clarendon Press.

Yúdice, G. (2003). *The expediency of culture: Uses of culture in the global era.* Durham, NC: Duke University Press.

Zelizer, V. (1985). *Pricing the priceless child: The changing social value of children.* New York: Basic Books.

INDEX